THE
SHORT
LIFE OF
HUGHIE
McLOON

THE
SHORT
LIFE OF
HUGHIE
M<small>c</small>LOON

A TRUE STORY OF

BASEBALL, MAGIC
AND MURDER

ALLEN ABEL

sh.
SUTHERLAND
HOUSE

TORONTO, 2020

Sutherland House
416 Moore Ave., Suite 205
Toronto, ON M4G 1C9

First hardcover edition, June 2020

If you are interested in inviting one of our authors to a live event or
media appearance, please contact publicity@sutherlandhousebooks.com
and visit our website at sutherlandhousebooks.com for more
information about our authors and their schedules.

Manufactured in the United States
Cover designed by Lena Yang
Book composed by Karl Hunt

Library and Archives Canada Cataloguing in Publication
Title: The short life of Hughie McLoon : a true story of baseball,
magic and murder / Allen Abel.
Names: Abel, Allen J., 1950- author.
Description: Includes index.
Identifiers: Canadiana 20200178792 | ISBN 9781989555217 (hardcover)
Subjects: LCSH: McLoon, Hughie. | LCSH: Philadelphia Athletics (Baseball team) |
LCSH: Bat boys—
Pennsylvania—Philadelphia—Biography. | LCSH: Mascots—
Pennsylvania—Philadelphia—Biography. |
LCGFT: Biographies.
Classification: LCC GV865.M378 A24 2020 |
DDC 796.357092—dc23

ISBN 978-1-989555-21-7

For Lizzie,
who will write
wonderful books someday,
but, hey, no pressure;

for Natasha,
who really likes baseball,
if you can drag her to the stadium;

and for Debbie,
in her Yankees cap,
who has always, always cared.

The deformed man is always conscious that the world does not expect very much from him . . . He becomes extraordinarily sensitive to other people's first impressions of him. Those who are to be his friends he knows instantly . . . This sensitiveness has both its good and bad sides. It makes friendship that most precious thing in the world.

—Randolph Silliman Bourne, "The Handicapped—
By One of Them," *Atlantic Monthly,* 1911

Signs, omens, dreams, predictions
Are not all fictions
And many facts does hist'ry cite,
Which show that I am right!
—*La Mascotte,* 1880

I tol' him I'd bring him luck, an' I did!
—Hughie McLoon

TABLE OF CONTENTS

CHAPTER ONE

"Idol"

HUGHIE MCLOON WALKED OUT of the speakeasy at a quarter to two in the morning with a hoodlum on each arm. Here he was, the most recognized and popular little guy in Philadelphia—hadn't they asked him to hold up the round cards at the Dempsey-Tunney fight with 130,000 people in the stands?—and now he was running his own café at Tenth and Cuthbert, five short blocks from Independence Hall and the Liberty Bell, and life should have been, as they said in those days, the berries.

McLoon was serving sandwiches, "light lunch," and bootleg ale and whisky ladled from buckets secreted behind the counter when two wise guys with names off a Hofbrau menu, Meister and Fries, imposed themselves. They were into their beer even before they'd hauled up and now, more having been applied, they began bragging loudly about things they'd done and girls they'd ravished and people they knew around town. Hughie decided to invite his guests into Philadelphia's summer air, lest the scene become more indecorous.

Just then a car, later identified (rather unhelpfully) as "a black machine" or "a big sedan," came busting down Arch Street. It swerved southbound on Tenth, and braked sharply in front of the three men. A gun poking through the left rear window ended the short life of Hughie McLoon.

The date was Thursday, August 9, 1928. Hughie was twenty-six years and nineteen days old. Part of his face and skull were blown away. The morning papers called it an accident. The gunman or gunmen, it was reported and widely accepted, had been aiming for the two ejected customers, low-ranking mugs whom they had been tailing all evening in hopes of a quick assassination, a couple of drinks, some light lunch, and early to bed. It was dark at Tenth and Cuthbert, and Hughie, however famous, however small a target at less than fifty inches and eighty pounds, was collateral damage.

After the shooting, the black machine "raced in wild excitement for blocks around" and disappeared. A pair of firemen from Engine Company 20, less than fifty yards from the massacre, heard the shots and ran toward the scene. They followed a river of blood down eight steps to the entrance of Devine's Shoe Repair. Hughie McLoon, the former mascot of the baseball Athletics, the lucky hunchback who tended the bats, "a cripple who basked in the shadow of the strong," the Dapper Dan about town who "lived in a heaven of his own construction," the crony of crime-busters and prizefighters and pull hitters and rumrunners alike, "the Hughie who loved the spotlight, the Hughie who loved the crowds," was lying there with more than a dozen wounds to the head, face, and body. In the mascot's pocket, the firemen found twenty-five cents.

Hughie's death wrung from a city inured to underworld violence after eight and a half years of Prohibition an outpouring worthy of the operatic stage. "In the circles in which he moved he was known to thousands," the *Philadelphia Record* grieved. "And a tragic end brought the throng closer to him in death than it had ever been in life."

But what of William Meister and Joseph Fries (whose real names, it turned out, were Liko and Belko)? The latter limped away with a slight wound to the calf. It was the second time he'd been shot in thirty-two days, and not the last.

Detectives brought Belko/Fries to City Hall and asked their questions, seeking to identify the men in the death car. "Yes, I know them," he said, "but believe me, I'm not going to squeal."

Poor Meister/Liko, meanwhile, having accumulated thirteen shotgun fragments in the legs, groin, and midsection, was deposited under police guard in the Jefferson Hospital "at the point of death." A last statement was solicited but the wounded man merely grinned and rolled over. "He is not expected to live," prophesied the Philadelphia *Evening Bulletin*. So dangerous were Meister's wounds that he would cling to life for only thirty more years.

But Hughie was gone. "McLoon Called Innocent Victim in Gang War," Philadelphia was told on Saturday morning, quoting police headquarters. "The little hunchback had no part in the racket which brews murder as well as booze," avowed the *Record*.

His body lay in state in a little row house on Shunk Street in South Philly, two blocks off Broad. At least fifteen thousand people shuffled through the August swelter to pay their respects, or just to stare. They saw a twisted, dark-haired little Irishman laid out in evening clothes, with a white aster in his buttonhole. "By some magical touch," the papers informed the multitudes who were turned away, "the evidences of the gunfire which tore out an eye and bored through his cheeks had been removed."

An incandescent crucifix lit the narrow parlor. A wreath at the head of the bier, one among hundreds sent by the luminaries of American League baseball, Pennsylvania politics, and organized crime, bore the single word: "Idol." It was from his mother.

"I warned Hughie often not to go into business up there," Elizabeth Palmer McLoon Geatens, a Madonna in black crepe, deposed between sobs, "but he always comforted me by saying he was well able to take care of himself. He was always so good to me."

In the corner of the dining room was a birdcage covered with a cloth.

"Look here," Mrs. Geatens said. "That's the last thing he bought me only a short time ago. Now I can't bear to raise the cloth from the cage and the poor bird wonders what's the matter. Oh, if my son had only stayed home last night."

The next morning, Hughie McLoon, in a full-length coffin, was lifted by two magistrates, a municipal hack, the University of Pennsylvania track coach, and a couple of lawyers into St. Monica's Church, and thence to Holy Cross Cemetery in Yeadon, where he would in time be joined by his mother, father, and half-sister under a sizable gray slab that reads, on its eastern side: "Former Mascot of the Athletics."

"Few of the really big men in public life are showered in death with such honors," one newspaperman commented, as the knell of civic grief was tolled. The entire cost of Hughie McLoon's funeral was met by Max "Boo Boo" Hoff, boxing impresario and (as-yet unsuspected) king of Philadelphia's million-bottle lawless liquor trade.

* * *

Hughie McLoon had vaulted onto the ball fields and the sports pages of Philadelphia in the terrible July of 1916, when, as a skinny, crippled, irrepressible eighth-grader at Our Lady of Mount Carmel School, he was cast for the role that would be carved into his head-stone a dozen summers later: the living talisman of the greatest baseball team in the universe.

That team was manager Connie Mack's Athletics, perennial champions of the American League, winners of four of the previous six league pennants and three World Series championships. How the team ascended, then fell, and why in 1916 the grieving, desperate players needed to call upon the fourteen-year-old McLoon, is a saga too sad and mystical to be untrue.

Its genesis lies in humanity's deepest superstitions, our yearning to bring a sense of control to lives riddled with uncertainty. Stir our unyielding, if ridiculous, faith in fairies, charms, and totems together with our competing feelings of pity, curiosity, and revulsion for the disabled and deformed, then combine them with the maddening difficulty of hitting a speeding, spinning sphere with a hickory bat, and the product is Hughie McLoon.

"I use'ta go to the ball park and watch the A's play," Hughie told an interviewer, relating his origin story as mascot of the Athletics. "Funny, huh?"

For McLoon, getting to Shibe Park was easy enough: his grandmother's house and his uncle's flat were right down West Lehigh Avenue from the stadium. Getting inside, to the clubhouse, the dugout, and into the players' hearts, was another matter.

A century ago, of all the heavens that a city boy could dream of, tending the bats for a big-league baseball club ranked at the top. But as Hughie discovered from his earliest Saturdays in the grandstand, to be the luckiest, you first had to be unlucky. Then you had to convince the gods of the diamond that the crucible of your own suffering rendered you a guardian against ill fortune.

As a young spectator at Shibe Park in the early 1910s, Hughie McLoon saw living proof that this could be done. Looking down from the twenty-five-cent seats upon the World Champions at work, the schoolboy McLoon, like hundreds of thousands of other Philadelphians, was a witness to the deeply intertwined lives of two men of extremes: mastermind Connie Mack and miniature Louis Van Zelst. One was the ballclub's manager and president. The other was the team's batboy, its mascot, and, many of the players believed, the secret to their success. One was tall and the other tiny; one mature and one adolescent; one vigorous and one frail; one stern and one gay. Mack was fated to prosper into his tenth decade; Van Zelst not to reach twenty-one, not truly to become a man at all.

It was baseball's Age of Magic, a time never to come again. Nine innings, four bases, three outs: the contest on the field would be familiar to anyone today. But the game also possessed a supernatural dimension that elevated Louis Van Zelst and Hughie McLoon and dozens of other outsiders—whether humpbacks, midgets, freaks, harlequins, or children of color—to the status of jujus in stadiums across the country. "Probably there are a million kids in this country who would swap their hope of eternal life to be in the shoes of little Louis Van Zelst," it was written in 1912. He was, one newspaper story blared, the "most envied boy in the country . . . the proudest kid in President Taft's dominions."

When the Athletics were at bat, Van Zelst would scrape out two shallow pits with his spikes between the A's bench and home plate. The paper's story continued: "Here he would squat and watch every move, as if he were Mack himself." And he chirruped to each man moving toward the batter's box: "Rub my hump! Better rub my hump for a hit this time! Rub my hump!"

Unfailingly, they touched him. Inscrutably, he touched them as well. Little Van was far from baseball's first hunchbacked mascot, and Hughie McLoon would not be the last.

From the vantage of this century, it was perverse and cruel. But from the Shibe Park grandstand in the 1910s, and on the field where the mighty Athletics flung and flailed, it was as real as a beanball.

"Funny, huh?"

* * *

"History is valuable, to begin with, because it is true," Bertrand Russell wrote in 1904, when Hughie was two. "To know how the world developed to the point at which our individual memory begins, how the religions, the institutions, the nations among which we live, became what they are; to be acquainted with the great of other times, with customs and beliefs differing widely from our own—these things are indispensable to any consciousness of our position."

What follows, however fantastical, is a real history of real people in the real city of Philadelphia. At its heart is Hughie McLoon, who left a vibrant and fascinating, if frustratingly incomplete trail. We can follow the fatherless McLoon, always hungry for the affection and companionship of important men, through his relationships with heavyweight boxers, playboy millionaires, baseball legends, and the Marine Corps general imported to dry up liquor-drenched Philadelphia. There are box scores of the ballgames he mascotted and church and civil records of his mother's and father's and stepfather's marriages and movements and gruesome deaths.

We can observe Hughie in the many jurisdictions in which he served during his short life, from Connie Mack's Athletics to the office of the state boxing commissioner to the sports department of the Philadelphia *Evening Public Ledger* and his own saloon on Cuthbert Street. Hughie knew all of these worlds, lived in them, suffered and strove and was loved in them before dying, before the age of thirty, two and one-half miles from the row-house in which he was born.

It is impossible to fill the blank spaces of chance and fortune, acceptance and rejection that colored McLoon's life. We have mere hints of the shattered family of his early childhood, of his long nights under the ring lights and in darkened bars, and of the nature of his effect on others, but sometimes they are brilliant hints. "He grins, and grins and grins some more and you, even though your wrath be frightful and mighty and your sorrows everwhelming (*sic*), look at that grin and grin back," a man named McCurley wrote of Hughie in 1922.

Hughie also has a knack, even when his own figure is indistinct, for illuminating the people and the world around him. The numinous hunchbacks, the Dancing Judge, the body-puncher who dined with Clifford Odets, the flapper-chasers, the anti-liquor firebreathers, the Hall of Famers, the double Medal of Honor awardee who handed the baubles back, the teenaged runaway in the bloodstained bed, the industrial distillers, the girl "checking coats" in the middle of summer, the publican Irish, the gangster Jews—all of them shared the same hour and walked streets named Broad and Cuthbert and Arch and Race. All knew Shibe Park and the Mummers' Parade on New Year's Day and the solid-stone, sky-scraping new city hall at the center of America's founding metropolis, with Penn himself, iron-cast and unblinking, at its crown. All lived through the deadly streetcar strike of 1910, the polio epidemic of 1916, the anti-black riots, the War to End All Wars, the Spanish Flu, and the great explosion at the Eddystone Ammunition Corporation that killed more than a hundred women and girls one awful April day. They were turbulent, violent years. Life was precarious and relatively cheap. Blind luck, for good or ill, wielded an influence we hardly recognize today, and it drives our story as much as all the human will in Philadelphia.

The characters are gone now, and several elapsed in excruciating ways: gun blasts, starvation, plummeting into the Niagara Gorge and subsequent amputation by the *Maid of the Mist*, tuberculosis, lung cancer in a police-guarded ward, a fractured skull from a tumble down the stairs ("Probably drunk," says the dead man's grandson). A son of Hughie's half-sister drove off the Ben Franklin Bridge on New Year's Eve. Another relative used to club his kids with a two-by-four if they were slow to bring him a highball.

However they departed, they are now mute, and the traces they left in interviews and affidavits are few. His were not the people that posterity cherishes. Fifteen years of searching have turned up no letters, no diary, no memoir, and no offspring of Hughie McLoon.

This story is based on what was reported publicly at the time, which may or may not be truth as per Russell. *The Front Page*, Ben Hecht's epic smackdown of creative, cutthroat newspapering, debuted on Broadway the day of Hughie's funeral, after all.

What we have is not complete but it is sufficient for us to become acquainted with Hughie's life and times, with the great and (unmentioned by Bertrand Russell) the not-so-great of Prohibition-era America, their customs and beliefs, differing so widely from our own, and to improve our consciousness of our own position.

And it is enough to address the lingering question: How could an American boy in a broken body who lived a leprechaun's life be fated to die a gangster's death? In 1930, a scandal sheet called *True Detective Mysteries* returned to Hughie's story. "Was it an unintentional slaying?" the magazine asked. "Were the death bullets meant for the two men who were standing by McLoon when he was killed?"

A century later, many everwhelming mysteries remain. Who would have wanted to kill the once most popular pupil from Our Lady of Mount Carmel School? What part was played by the gangsters' molls—"those furtive, bright-eyed creatures, sometimes pretty, but usually not?"

"Who," asked *True Detective Mysteries*," was the intended target on the night the bullets flew?"

CHAPTER TWO

"Unwholesome-Looking Children"

N OCTOBER 1896, a reporter from the *Philadelphia Inquirer* walked two blocks from the newspaper's headquarters to a disquieting scene at the Lower Delaware Hotel, just inland from the river that has been the city's artery for more than two hundred years. Workmen, the reporter discovered, were taking a battle-ax to George Washington's old boudoir.

"Big yawning fireplaces that date back to Revolutionary times are to be torn out of the historic little tavern and the hand of progress is to be ruthlessly laid upon the old rooms," the reporter lamented:

> Washington was a guest here many times, and the little second-story front room looking out to busy Second Street is still known to residents in the vicinity as Washington's Hall. Jefferson, Franklin, Robert Morris, Dr. Rush and nearly every other noted man of the post-Revolutionary epoch is known to have stopped here.
>
> Fortunately, the house itself is to remain, and its present proprietor, Hugh McLoon, is imbued with such respect for the

historic association of the place that he will preserve as much of the antique fittings and flavor as possible.

Enter the Philadelphia McLoons, sometimes styled McLoone, McLloon, McGloon, or even Macaloon, sons of Donegal, fathers of short-lived Pennsylvanians, and heirs to the extraordinary, experimental republic that Thomas Jefferson declared and Benjamin Franklin elegized and General Washington defended, right here in what William Penn himself intended to be a "Greene Country Towne." In 1896, the McLoons had only just arrived. By 1928, nearly all of them would be gone.

The preservationist and taverner of Second Street was cousin Hugh Patrick McLoon, a liquor purveyor who took part in Democratic Party politics, sat as a commissioner of the Mummers Parade (in 1907, he would vote against allowing women to be judges of costumes and floats) and served at Quarter Sessions Court as a "tipstaff," a uniquely Pennsylvanian description for a minor jurisprudential position.

Already, at the turn of the twentieth century, Philadelphia publicans such as Hughie's cousin were being wetted by the first waves of the great tsunami of self-righteousness that would eventually crest over the nation in the form of Prohibition. In 1903, Hugh P. McLoon paid the city treasury the sum of $1,103 to transfer his liquor license from Washington's Hall to another joint on East Girard Avenue but the seller reneged, vowing that no property of his would be used to sell the devil's nectar. "McLoon," noted the trade publication *American Bottler*, "has decided not to go into the liquor business after all and his friends in the city councils have passed a bill to reimburse him to the extent of one thousand dollars for the unused license."

The McLoons were unimaginative when choosing names for their sons. Batboy Hughie's grandfather was Hugh McLoone with an "e," although he marked his name with an "x." He died and left his earthly estate to his widow, Mary Munday McLoon. She had two sons, one Hugh F., the other Daniel; and Daniel had one child, the mascot Hughie.[1]

The matrilineal contribution began with a Navy man named David Palmer, who sailed as a rigger through some of the most titanic coastal battles of the Civil War. He and his wife, Julia, had four children, including a girl named Elizabeth, or Lizzie. Their home was at the corner of Reed and Leithgow Streets, steps from the Church of Our Lady of the Sacred Heart. An afternoon photograph from that period, looking northward up Leithgow, shows cart tracks and hoofprints in a sandy lane lined by three-story row houses with shutters wide and windows open.

In January 1901, twenty-one-year-old Daniel McLoon, who had recently been working as a clerk, possibly for his cousin Hugh P. at the Lower Delaware Hotel, was listed as living with his sainted, widowed mother, Mary, in North Philadelphia. Soon after, he appeared in the public records of the Irish immigrant enclave of Gloucester City, New Jersey as the civil-union, but not church-blessed groom of Miss Elizabeth Palmer, daughter of Able Seaman David Palmer.

The new Mrs. McLoon also cited a Gloucester City address on the marriage form. And that is all we have. There is no surviving account of how these suspiciously hasty interstate nuptials were concocted, or what the bridesmaids wore. On the affidavit, Daniel McLoon listed his residence as 204 Orange Street, but no such dwelling exists on the 1901 Gloucester City plats. The whole thing smells a bit off: the fake address, a ceremony performed by a justice of the peace in an insurance office across the river from home, with two strangers as witnesses and no family members noted as present—a queer first step on the path to connubial bliss.

---

1   If this is confusing, keep in mind that the San Francisco Giants once started an outfield of Alou, Alou, and Alou.

By autumn, Lizzie had conceived, President William McKinley had been assassinated at the Pan-American Exposition in Buffalo, Teddy Roosevelt was in the White House, and the novice Mrs. McLoon was ferrying back to Pennsylvania to be nearer her kin. Whether Daniel sailed with her, and whether their marriage was real or just the impulse of two frightened, hot-blooded kids, is unknowable.

Lizzie's baby was born at home on July 21, July 28, or August 1, 1902, depending on whether you trust the infant's baptismal record at Holy Cross, a hastily scrawled death certificate ("Cause: Gun Shot") from August 1928, or Hughie himself, who always talked up July 21 as his birthday.

At the end of 1902, Daniel McLoon was back with mother Mary in North Philly, and it is reasonable to assume that Elizabeth was now a single mother in residence with her own parents and siblings on Leithgow St., two hours away by trolley car from the infant's absent father.

The details of Lizzie and Daniel's relationship are not important; he will shortly be dead of tuberculosis. Even before he succumbs, she will be pregnant again, by a young scrap-metal dealer and war veteran from the shady side of Leithgow Street.

* * *

Philadelphia, on the Opening Day of the Progressive Era, was the third-largest city in the United States of America (and it would remain so until overtaken by Los Angeles in the 1950s). Its institutions, monuments, libraries, universities, mansions, churches and chambers, its fame-cracked bells and defiant we-hold-these-truths credentials, ranked it highly among the world's capitals of liberty, courage, and honor. But all of that grandeur and history reposed in Philadelphia's core, Center City, in the shade of William Penn's famous hat.

Hughie McLoon was born further south, in a rats' nest of a neighborhood vividly described by the physician Arthur Ames Bliss, who made horse-drawn house calls there and considered the people to whom he dispensed his charitable services sub-human. He saw:

> . . . two young, ill favored, hangdog-looking men, both of whom will probably be jailed or hung in the course of time and justice . . . a young woman who, like most of the women of the neighborhood, was probably common property of all the men . . . uncanny, deformed and unwholesome-looking children who amble to the gutter's edge and make uncouth gestures as we pass.
>
> Evil-faced things in men's clothing creep along the walls and glare at us with stupid, brutish eyes. The street is rank with filth, which is strewn everywhere. Through the gutters, which are so full that they overflow their channels, moves a sluggish mass of thick, opaque fluid in which floats decaying animal and vegetable matter.
>
> It was all part of their everyday lives. They had never been clean, and never desired to cultivate the state of cleanliness. The very ground seems alive with humanity. It pours up out of dark cellars, out of narrow courts. The houses on either side are literally packed and swarming with mankind. Up this way I go, till, arriving at a still more unsightly hole at the rear of the main house, I knock . . .

These exemplars of wretched refuse were mostly new, legal, white immigrants and, in the words of one noted scholar, "largely poor."[2]

---

2   Of the major East Coast cities, Philadelphia had the fewest foreign-born residents, barely 20 percent as the century began. Its population had been stagnant for decades, although this would change as new immigrants arrived in steerage aboard steam-powered caravans originating in Russia, eastern Europe, and Italy.

Appalled as Dr. Bliss was by South Philadelphia, others were just as disgusted by the inner workings of Center City, despite its magnificent opera and concert halls and its retail palaces. Proper Philadelphians might have been enraptured by cricket as much as baseball. They might have rowed manfully on the Schuylkill, exhibited their daughters at the diamond-studded Assemblies (founded in 1748), given the world hard iron, soft carpets, and Breyer's Ice Cream, but they also enabled a politics of such unabashed partisan thuggery, bribery, and graft that nobody in City Hall even blinked when, in July 1903, journalist Lincoln Steffens reported that "other American cities, no matter how bad their own condition may be, all point to Philadelphia as worse—'the worst-governed city in the country.'"

Steffens's essay in *McClure's Magazine,* entitled "Corrupt and Contented," was part and pinnacle of his rigorously sourced exposé of civic malfeasance across America. "The honest citizens of Philadelphia have no more rights at the polls than the negroes down South," he sneered. "Nor do they fight very hard for this basic privilege."

In *McClure's,* Steffens detailed a polling station set up in a whorehouse, and voting lists that included "dead dogs, children, and non-existent persons." He noted a speech by a ward heeler in a part of the city where many of the founding fathers once resided. The orator invoked the guest list of immortals from the Lower Delaware Hotel, H. McLoon, proprietor: "These men, the fathers of American liberty, voted here once!" he winked. "And they vote here yet!"

If anything, the muckraker understated the corruption. Two decades later, an investigative committee of the United States Senate estimated that the average Philadelphia elector had only a one-in-eight chance of having his ballot accurately canvassed, properly collected, and actually credited to the man he voted for.

* * *

Down on Leithgow Street, meanwhile, Elizabeth Palmer McLoon had a new neighbor, a twenty-two-year-old Irishman named Peter Geatens who had been honorably discharged from the U.S. Army after serving with the 3rd Infantry, far across the Pacific.

Forgotten today, the so-called Philippine Insurrection in which Private Geatens saw a few weeks of combat is a flyspeck in the nation's military history. But the sporadic, racialist, three-year conflict, which lasted from 1899 to 1902 after the 1898 U.S. victory in the Spanish-American War, was a fierce and pitiless series of reciprocal massacres, group hangings, ethnic cleansings, village burnings, ambuscades, slogs, and atrocities, waged against a determined, patriotic enemy in the swamps and labyrinthine cane-fields that they called home. On the Fourth of July, seventeen days before Hughie was born, President Roosevelt declared victory in this noble cause, called Geatens and the 3rd Infantry home, and offered the treacherous supposed rebels what he termed a "wise and humane" amnesty "conducive to peace, order, and loyalty among them."

After his discharge, Peter Geatens strode up Reed Street, turned north on Leithgow to visit his brother Dan at number 1304, and noticed a lovely young lady rocking a newborn baby on her stoop across the street at 1311, no husband in sight. We can guess the rest, but we never can know what inner demons a soldier carries home in his kit. No one in the living family remembers a kind word being spoken about Peter Geatens.

By the time Hughie turned three, his birth father had been diagnosed with TB. His mother, already going abroad as Elizabeth Geatens without benefit of a formal union, was living with her ex-soldier on what would be a succession of South Philadelphia side streets. In her womb, she carried a girl that she and Peter would name Dorothy.

The hour of Dorothy Geatens's conception can be backdated to July 1905, Hughie's fourth summer: for lucky boys a wondrous season of first friends and daring dashes through sandboxes and puddles, and laughing home to mother's waiting arms. There is no reason to consider Hughie among the fortunate. He may have spent his time in a yard at Our Lady of the Holy Cross on Reed Street, or south in Mifflin Square, or a few blocks up Leithgow at a haunted quadrant called Weccacoe. For a playmate, he had the slightly older Jennie Morozzi of Earp Street, remembered (much later) by Elizabeth Geatens for her meltdowns and wild shrieks.

The children's park at Weccacoe Square hid a shameful history. In 1897, the sociologist W.E.B. Du Bois was invited by the University of Pennsylvania to undertake a study of Philadelphia's forty thousand African Americans, "a people," he noted, "comparatively low on the scale of civilization." There were few other cases in the history of civilized peoples, Du Bois wrote in *The Philadelphia Negro*, "where human suffering has been viewed with such peculiar indifference."[3] What struck Du Bois most starkly was what he called "the curious prejudice of whites not to allow Negroes to be buried near their dead." Segregation, even in the tomb. Denied eternal rest among the lighter-skinned, many Philadelphia blacks were buried in the Bethel Burying Ground at Weccacoe Square. By 1830, a total of 1,716 interments had been registered. Perhaps another three thousand coffins were piled right atop their ancestors' caskets before the cemetery was abandoned in 1864 and used as an equipment yard for a sugar refinery.

At the turn of the century, the city took over the block and Weccacoe became a softball field and playground with basketball nets, a ring-toss area, a punching bag, a seesaw, and the dead below.

3   Du Bois, W.E.B., *The Philadelphia Negro: A Social Study* (Eastford, Martino Fine Books, 2017).

It was in all likelihood to Weccacoe that Elizabeth Geatens or Jennie Morozzi or some aunt or neighbor brought three-year-old Hughie McLoon in the summer of 1905, changing the trajectory of his life. Amid the playground shrieks and laughter, he fell from the see-saw and sprawled broken in the dirt. They lifted his shattered body off the ground and carried him away as the streetcars trundled down toward Mount Carmel, ringing their bells.

CHAPTER THREE

"The Base-Ball Fever"

THE PHILADELPHIA ATHLETICS were six runs behind the Cleveland Bronchos after six and a half innings at the Columbia Avenue Grounds on the day their future bat-boy was born. The home team, somehow inspired, battled back in the bottom of the seventh. The A's left fielder and leadoff man, the undersized, speedy Tully F. "Topsy" Hartsel, crushed a two-run homer. Cleveland committed two errors in the outfield and muffed a grounder to let in four more runs, and suddenly the game was tied.

In the dugout was the angular Cornelius McGillicuddy, the A's teetotalling and devoutly Roman Catholic field manager, general manager, and owner, called Connie Mack since childhood. The son of an Irish immigrant laborer and wheelwright, he was born in Massachusetts during the first winter of the Civil War and made his name as a pencil-thin catcher in the days before the introduction of the wire mask, chest protector, and shin guards. When Mack was young, the catcher would stand well behind the batter and take the ball on a bounce, so as not to get killed by a foul to the face. Now thirty-nine years old, a widower and father of three, six years removed from his playing career, Mack would rely on his bullpen to keep the Bronchos off the bases.

The Athletics and the American League were only a year and a half old but the A's were already known as "the Mackmen."[4] Mack scouted, hired, trained, and stole players of surpassing power, skill and creativity, giving America's virtuous old colonial capital its last illusion of eminence over dissolute New York. No one knew the intricacies of baseball positioning and strategy better. Mack, in fact, invented many of them.

Needing two innings of scoreless relief, Mack then turned to his left-handed pitching ace Rube Waddell, the unhittable and perhaps autistic fire-engine chaser, cocktail shaker, vaudeville actor, and alligator wrestler. The Rube delivered.

In the bottom of the ninth, Hartsel led off with a single. He stole second base. He stole third. Then, with two out, A's catcher Ossee Schrecongost, himself a former batboy and Waddell's preferred battery (and drinking) partner—in fact, one of few adults who could focus Rube on the task of firing a ball past a man with a bat over a seventeen-inch slab for money—cracked a single to score Topsy and win the game, 11–10, a fitting birthday present for their future mascot.

On July 21, 1902, the Mackmen and Bronchos required only two hours and five minutes to score twenty-one runs, make thirty-one hits, and employ five pitchers. A rookie umpire named Francis "Silk" O'Loughlin worked the game alone. Lemonade was a nickel, pretzels a penny each. "Urbane and gentlemanly agents pass among the crowd," reported the Philadelphia newspaper the *North American*,

---

4   Mack's reign as a major-league field manager would extend from 1894 until 1950, when the kindly, crackly, confused, 88-year-old Towering Tactician—"The Grand Old Man of the Grand Old Game"—having suffered what may have been a series of mini-strokes, having not won a pennant in twenty years, and still wearing his wool suit, starched collar, and necktie on the bench each day, finally retires: "I'm not quitting because I'm too old," he insists, "but because I think the people want me to."

"calling attention to their 'clean' ham sandwiches." There was no alcohol for sale, legally (Philadelphia stadiums would not serve beer until 1961). The Athletics' 2,409 fans poured out of the splintery stands and crossed the street into the non-air-conditioned pubs, delirious.

At sundown, the A's were in third place in the American League standings. The correspondent for the *Philadelphia Inquirer*, Frank Hough, who just happened to own, along with Mr. Mack, a share of the A's franchise, sensed destiny on this day of miraculous events:

> There's no denying it. These Athletics are a tough bunch to beat. On many occasions this season they have given evidence of the fact that they are never beaten until the last man has been retired in the ninth inning . . .
>
> After the Athletics had tied the score in their half of the seventh, Manager Mack concluded to take no chances, so he sent in the invincible Reuben Waddell . . .

Waddell's name was not Reuben. It was George, and he was only invincible when available. He vanished for days at a time, to fish or tend bar in Camden, New Jersey. Recently, it had taken two Pinkerton detectives in Connie Mack's employ two weeks to drag Waddell east from California, where he had been pitching for a team called the Los Angeles Loo Loos, and into Columbia Park, where, when leading with two out in the ninth inning, he was known to shout, "Send the crowd home, it's all over!"

* * *

Professional league baseball was only a quarter-century old at the hour of Hughie McLoon's birth but everything beautiful about the game already was in place: the *hurry, Dad* walk with the crowd from the streetcar; the sudden, perfect green of the grass against the city's grime; the filling grandstand and joshing athletes in their monogrammed flannels; the hurling, the slugging, the sliding, the roaring, the heckling; the game's deep lode of custom, statistics, and lore.

Baseball was recognized as a purely American confection, despite its British ancestry. "Well," wrote Walt Whitman, "the hurrah! game; it's our game: that's the chief fact in connection with it: America's game: has the snap, go, fling, of the American atmosphere—belongs as much to our institutions, fits into them as significantly, as our constitutions, laws: is just as important in the sum total of our historic life."

By 1876, cities great and picayune swelled and swooned with their hired nines. Top players earned top dollar and enjoyed local fame. The mustachioed masculinity of the athletes left large numbers of female fans hot under the parasol. In the City of Brotherly Love, baseball was so universally enjoyed that even its most afflicted citizens competed with pride and ginger.

"One-legged base-ball players will contend with one-armed batsmen," proclaimed a headline in the *Philadelphia Times*, April 20, 1883:

> The base-ball fever has attacked the cripples. Two teams have been made up entirely of maimed men.
>
> A. Hanson is the pitcher. An accident in a rolling mill cost him his left arm from the elbow down. J. Flick guards third base. His right arm was amputated at the shoulder after a car had run over it. William Young is left fielder. A cannon ball carried his right hand and wrist away at the battle of Gettysburg . . .
>
> All of the "Hoppers" lost their legs while working on railroads . . .

The game's popularity masked its less appealing facets, including rampant game-fixing, virulent racism, lifetime contractual bondage, players staggering around drunk during games, and rubbing a teen-aged hunchback's deformity (or a young African American's head) for luck on the way to home plate. Most players' salaries were minimal, illicit gambling was universal—Rube Waddell was known to leap into the stands to pummel taunting bettors—and the corporate structure of the two major leagues virtually defined the word "monopsony."

The popularity of the professional game had led to the creation of the American League in 1901, touching off a plunder. The new AL teams filled their rosters with stars from the entrenched National League, contracts be damned. Connie Mack found himself at war with John Joseph McGraw, the profane and brilliant rival manager whose National League New York Giants, a few years later, would face the A's in the seminal World Series (plural) of the Age of Magic.

"There was a time when I thought that McGraw was a baseball man," Mack sneered after McGraw accused the American League of being on the verge of bankruptcy and dissolution. "But since I have been closely associated with him, I have been compelled to change that opinion." McGraw countered by defaming the Athletics as a "white elephant," an epithet that Mack converted into a logo that the A's, even when resident in Oakland, California, still wear on their uniforms more than a century later.

As the professional game became more popular, success in the batter's box became more and more difficult. "The hardest thing to do in sports is to hit a round baseball with a round bat, squarely," Ted Williams of the Red Sox observed in the 1940s, but this axiom was valid long before his time. Through the 1880s and 1890s, as players adopted leather gloves to cushion the sting of hard drives, as infields became better groomed and less unpredictable, as strikes were counted against the batsman even if he did not swing, and as underhand pitching was replaced by smoking fastballs, disgusting spitters, and diabolical curves, everything about getting a hit became harder. Then, as now, making one single in every three turns at bat qualified a man as an all-star. Twice in five rendered him immortal.

With the dawning century came still more obstacles to hits. The pitcher's mound was created. Foul balls were counted as strikes. Rube Waddell invented his befuddling four-pump windmill windup, and the numerous dirty tricks devised in the 1880s by the young catcher Connie Mack caught on with other players. In his first professional seasons in Milwaukee, Buffalo, and Washington, Mack had been proficient in illegally nudging the hitter's bat as he was about to swing, and imitating the flicking sound of a caught foul tip when the batter had missed the ball entirely. A solitary umpire could not possibly keep up with runners being tripped and tackled behind his back, and other heinous deeds.

The baseball itself was so mushy and battered that it never flew too far. Bunts and choked-up bloops were the coin of the dead-ball age. A Chicago team so feeble that it was nicknamed the Hitless Wonders would win the 1906 World Series. And it became clear to everyone that the only sure antidote to failure was magic.

* * *

By the time Hughie McLoon was a month old, the American League A's had stolen everything from the National League Phillies, their hometown rivals, except home plate, and were clawing toward first place while outdrawing their neighbors three to one, and sometimes ten to one.

By mid-August, the Athletics, with Rube Waddell on course to win twenty-four games in little more than half a season, were in the lead to stay. In early September, the team's train collided with a Wabash freight somewhere east of St. Louis and not a player was scratched—the baseball gods were with them. The A's returned home to attract seventeen thousand fans to a doubleheader at Columbia

Grounds on September 10, competing for the AL pennant against the St. Louis Browns. Thousands hugged the foul lines and trampled the outfield grass. Waddell won both games in relief. The Phillies, at home on the same afternoon, drew 172.

On the night of September 30, 1902, in the most corrupt but joyous city in the United States of America, Connie Mack's White Elephants were paraded down Broad Street in a horse-drawn barouche past "a mammoth line of humanity, ablaze with red fire and resplendent in gorgeous costume," to "emblazon on history's pages the greatest athletic pageant in the history of the game."

"Philadelphia, slanderously referred to as slow by critics who know no better, cast dignity to the winds and let herself loose with a vengeance," said the *Inquirer*. "And why not? There was Rube Waddell, the mighty Rube, he of the strong arm, surrounded by his colleagues. The crowd went fairly wild."

So many spools of confetti were thrown from windows that marchers and horses alike were tripped and tangled, and one deputy sheriff, tossed from his mount, suffered "several severe contusions." Still, said the *Inquirer*, "The police arrangements were perfect." Baby Hughie McLoon had picked the best city in the world in which to be born and make his fame.

As for the beloved Rube Waddell, a crowd of admirers presented him with a gold pocket watch worth a staggering $165. A week later, in another crush of fans, somebody stole it.

In just a few weeks, Waddell would take a shot at playing professional football for a fledgling venture managed by Connie Mack. His career was short-lived: Rube was removed from the team after breaking his own quarterback's leg in a scrimmage. The next baseball season, he would strike out 302 men, and follow up with 349 the season after that, even as opposing coaches lay shiny objects along the baselines to distract his eye. In 1905, he would be accused of taking a bribe (never proved) to sit out the World Series against John

McGraw's Giants. After the 1907 season, in the same week that five-year-old Hughie's birth father died, Mack would sell Waddell to the St. Louis Browns for the price of a clean ham sandwich.

In 1913, the invincible Rube, born on Friday the Thirteenth, a boy who never had a day of formal schooling, "more sinned against than sinned," in Connie Mack's words, will exhaust himself while rescuing flood victims from the swollen Mississippi River in Hickman, Kentucky, develop pneumonia, then tuberculosis and, on April Fool's Day, die.

CHAPTER FOUR

"A Mascot!"

"WHEN HUMP-BACK occurs in children before the body has completed its growth, the legs and arms attain full size, but the body will not grow correspondingly at the spine; these parts are arrested in their development," wrote Hippocrates, circa 380 BC.

Two millennia later, in July 1900, a four-year-old named Leon Abeomontz was carried to University Hospital, Philadelphia by his despairing parents, "deserving Polish people," the *Philadelphia Inquirer* reported, who "boast but very few worldly possessions." The boy would be treated for "the deplorable deformity known as 'hunchback,' or, in scientific parlance, curvature of the spine."

Diagnosed with ankylosing spinal caries, "Little Leon's pale face and wasted form told a silent story of suffering, and the specialists who gathered around his cot gravely shook their heads. When he entered the hospital, Leon Abeomontz was a pitiable object."

A rotogravure with the story shows the tiny patient strapped to a bunk with a leather helmet on his skull and a lead weight attached by a pulley to the headgear. Little had changed since Hippocrates had lashed patients with kyphotic postures to a ladder and used stones to stretch their spines, or had a slave stand fixedly on the hump to press it down.

"Spine disease occurs chiefly in children and young adults, and is more frequently among boys than girls," the *Inquirer* explained. "A fall or a heavy blow are usually accountable for its origin . . . The children of impoverished parents are the most susceptible." But tuberculosis also could lead to spinal curvature, and TB was everywhere.

A sickly child, Leon had grown more and more emaciated. His parents initially thought him delicate. "Finally," said the *Inquirer,* "the realization of his true state forced itself upon them. The frail spine, suffering under the burden it was forced to bear, gave way. Leon was a hunchback!"

There is no record of how three-year-old Hughie was treated when he fell off the seesaw, if he was treated at all. The well-publicized case of Leon Abeomontz is our best approximation of what might have been done to help him. After eleven months in bed in his cowhide beanie with the weight hanging from the pulley stretching his thoracolumbar regions, Leon's hump began to shrink. When he entered the clinic, his condition had been assayed as "almost fatally serious." By June 1901, "though still slightly deformed, he is now a strong little fellow, rapidly outgrowing the deadly disease that would either have claimed him as an early victim or made him an incurable hunchback for life."

Whether Leon Abeomontz went on to a career of activity and health, or relapsed and died, no record exists. Not a single individual bearing his deserving Polish surname could be found in any directory in the United States in 2020. In 1912, "a new method for treating curvature of the spine or hunchback" was announced at the Congress of Surgeons in New York. A physician from Portland, Maine, "described an operation in which a piece of bone from a patient's leg was grafted to the spine thus relieving the necessity of braces and effecting a permanent cure."

No such remedy was performed on Hughie McLoon. It would take his mother seven years to teach her son to walk again after his fall in the playground.

* * *

At Fontainebleau in 1525, or thereabouts, the beloved Triboulet, hunchbacked court jester of King Francis I, made a move on another man's mistress. In the words of Rabelais, Triboulet was "properly and totally and fatally crazy," a sixteenth-century Rube Waddell: *"céleste, jovial, mercuriel, lunatique, erratique, excentrique, héroïque, et genial."*

"Admiral Chabot is going to murder me," the joker told the king.

"If he does such a thing, I will have him hanged within fifteen minutes," said the sovereign.

"Couldn't you have him hanged fifteen minutes before?" asked Triboulet.

The wise and celestial kyphotic, the lucky midget, the ornamental dwarf are all part of a macabre cult of littleness sweeping human history from the stumpy god Bes of the Egyptians to the "lucky hunchback" mosaic at ancient Antioch to Tyrion Lannister in *A Game of Thrones.*[5] They serve many cultural purposes, the little people.

Art critic Daniel A. Siedell writes of the Baroque masterpieces of Diego Velásquez, "it is possible to look at these dignified and

---

5 In 2004, when the Boston Red Sox finally won a World Series for the first time in 86 years, a good luck fixture in their clubhouse was a Dominican actor named Nelson de la Rosa, the shortest man in the world. Something in the ichor of normally-sized people must compel this need for contrast with the littlest of all.

insightful portraits of dwarfs as representative of the human condition, stripped of its pretense of beauty, honor, strength, wealth . . . The dwarf discloses the human condition more honestly and directly than kings, dukes, and ambassadors."

Loving and misunderstood, Victor Hugo's Quasimodo wastes away in a graveyard, embracing the earthly remains of his Esmerelda.

Conniving and cynical, the accursed Rigoletto hears his own daughter's death cries.

In George Eliot's *The Mill on the Floss,* the gentle, dreaming, hunchbacked Philip Wakem is accosted by the brother of his beloved Maggie, and warned:

> If you dare to make the least attempt to come near her, or to write to her, or to keep the slightest hold on her mind, your puny, miserable body, that ought to have put some modesty into your mind, shall not protect you. I'll thrash you; I'll hold you up to public scorn. Who wouldn't laugh at the idea of your turning lover to a fine girl?[6]

Meanwhile, for real-life little people, acceptance could be almost unattainable. In 1863, Lavinia Warren married P.T. Barnum's prized dwarf, General Tom Thumb, in Manhattan. By 1906, she was sixty-five years old and still two feet, eight inches tall. She recalled meeting presidential candidate Stephen A. Douglas, who stooped to kiss her as if she were a child: "It seemed impossible, to make people understand at first that I was not a child; that, being a woman I had the womanly instinct of shrinking from a form of familiarity which in the case of a child of my size would have been as natural as it was permissible."

---

6   Eliot, George, *The Mill on the Floss* (New York, Penguin Classics, 2003).

* * *

The impossible, yet real big-league baseball careers of disabled children such as Louis Van Zelst and Hughie McLoon, and many, many other batboys and mascots, originated in the confluence of three separate streams of culture that joined in the 1880s, the first being the disability itself.

"The doors of the deformed man are always locked, and the key is on the outside," testified the scholar Raymond Bourne in 1911. Bourne possessed both a humped back from tuberculosis and a deformed skull and ear, the results of a forceps injury and a twisted umbilicus. "When one is in full possession of his faculties, and can move about freely, bearing simply a crooked back and an unsightly face, his road is apt to be hard and rugged . . . For he has all the battles of a stronger man to fight, and he is at a double disadvantage in fighting them."

In this way, being a hunchback a century and more ago subsumed all the other types of identity that a person might have. Its bearer, to the superstitious, became the karmic equal of a shaman or a Gypsy or a Hindu *fakir*. The hump was thought to convey certain paranormal properties, including an ability to prestidigitate a rabbit's foot into a magic amulet simply by dismembering the rodent by moonlight in a cemetery.

Humans being human, not everyone saw humps as good omens. Their bearers were often subjected to unbearable taunting and ridicule. A Rhode Island newspaper reported in the 1880s:

Three deaths are now the result of the quarrel between clerks on Friday evening in the office of the Brown & Sharp Manufacturing Company. To the two victims shot by Fitzroy Willard have been added his father, who lies dead from heart failure following the shock of the news of his son's death . . .

The shooting resulted from the teasing to which Willard has been subjected on account of his hunchback brother . . .

A Charleston, West Virginia event produced this headline about a ten-year-old boy who could not stand the teasing: "Tormented hunchback kills baiter in duel; Boys fight with sharp pokers; one stabbed through heart."

Pottsville, Pennsylvania: "Hunchback crushed to death: mistaken for dog."

The second stream was baseball itself, a game that, with every innovation, became more and more difficult, frustrating, and fickle, especially for the hitter. Complicated rituals developed regarding the placement, storage, and curation of the bats, as if singles, doubles, triples, and home runs were cached like DNA within the wood itself. The fine Phillies' infielder Monte Cross later would become a member of the A's 1902 pennant winners:

One of Monte Cross' queer hobbies is that the bats must not be crossed when they lie in front of the bench. Yesterday, just as Wolverton, the first man up in the fifth inning, stepped to the plate, Cross looked at the pile of bats, at once jumped into the air, shouting "Four runs this time. It's a cinch. Never failed yet."

"Sit down. You're crazy," said Maul.

"I tell you we're going to get four runs this time. Do you see that?" he asked, pointing to the pile of bats.

"See what?"

"Why those four bats sticking out further than the rest. That means we'll get just that many runs. Just wait and see."

Everybody coughed, but Monte was evidently very much in earnest, so they waited, all thinking how they'd kid him when the side was out. Then Wolverton made a hit.

"It's the starter," said Cross. "Now watch me." But Cross aired to Donlin. Then the next man walked.

"There's four hits coming sure," said Cross.

Just then Thomas cracked a single, scoring Wolverton. Then Lajoie and Flick got in their work, and the four runs were scored.

"Whenever you see the bats crossed that way, look out for runs," said Cross, triumphantly.

"All right," replied McFarland, "shove out about six of those sticks and we'll win, sure."

"That doesn't go. Don't touch 'em, for heaven's sake," fairly screamed Cross. "The bat boy has to do it when he isn't thinking."

The players all had a good laugh over the circumstance, and, no doubt, some of them became converts to Monte's baseball religion.

A member of the Louisville Colonels spoke in 1886 about the dangers of packing up bats before a game was finished. "No matter how the score stands at the time," he said, "your luck is sure to flop right over and give the victory to the other side." He illustrated his certainty with an anecdote about a game against the Pittsburgh Alleghenys that the opponents led 10–5 with one inning left to play:

Victory looked so sure for the Pittsburghs that Pete Meegan, an extra man belonging to that team, who was sitting on the bench, begin packing up the bats when the last inning was commenced. You may not believe it, but it's an actual fact and a matter of record: our luck changed from that instant. (Louisville won 11–10.) Manager Phillips of the Pittsburghs was crazy with rage, but he didn't blame any of his players. He could have murdered Meegan, though, for bringing on a jonah [curse] by packing up those bats before the game had finished." Meegan never plays in the major leagues again.

The third stream arrived in North America via a delightful *opéra comique* that premiered in Paris in 1880, and soon crossed the Atlantic in English translation. Its title contained a word previously unknown outside southern France, and its premise was based on a Provençal folk legend—the novel idea that *une mascotte* could be more than a necklace or a ring or a coin or a dog or a goat or a mouse or the pedal extremity of a rabbit. It could be a human being.

As the action in Edmond Audran's *La Mascotte* begins, Prince Laurent XVI is visiting a farm during a hunt and bemoaning his ill fortune to Rocco, a humble tiller of the soil who is also dogged by bad luck.[7] Laurent sings:

> Signs, omens, dreams, predictions
> are not all fictions
> And many facts does hist'ry cite,
> which show that I am right!

The prince and Rocco begin to talk.

> ROCCO: What can trouble the existence of my prince?
> LAURENT: What is the trouble? Ill luck! I am doomed to misfortune! If I go to battle, I am generally beaten along the whole line. If I play at throwing dice, I invariably lose. If I aim at a deer, I kill a rabbit—that is, when I kill anything!
> ROCCO: The same with me. I have taken one thousand, one hundred and twenty-five tickets in the Sicilian lottery, and what have I won? A toothbrush, and a pair of buttons. Now if I had had a *mascotte* . . .
> LAURENT: You could have taken one ticket, and drawn the first prize—a fortune!

7   Audran, Edmond, La Mascotte (Patala Press, 2015)

Enter the pretty maid Bettina, a turkey wrangler and congenital *mascotte*. Bettina has been sent to Rocco, against her will, by Rocco's well-off and lucky brother, Antonio. Antonio hopes that Bettina will counter Rocco's bad luck. Rocco is overjoyed: "A *mascotte*! At last I possess a *mascotte*! Everything will succeed with me now! I shall buy lands and vineyards and stock. I shall become the richest farmer in the kingdom!" His happiness is then tempered by discovering a pamphlet of terms and conditions that, apparently, all *mascottes* carry.

Prince Laurent reads the tract aloud:

LAURENT: A Mascot should never marry other than a Mascot; for should a Mascot marry otherwise, all good influences will absolutely cease with the first bridal kiss.

ROCCO (shocked): The first bridal kiss!

LAURENT: We must watch her closely. No elopements or secret marriages in this case. Eternal vigilance will be the price of our future welfare!

After two more acts and numerous *drôle* turns of events, Bettina ditches Rocco and Laurent and marries her true love, the peasant Pippo.[8]

PIPPO: What luck! What chance! So I have married a *mascotte!*

ROCCO (stopping him, as he is about to enter the bedchamber): Unfortunate man, don't go there!

PIPPO: Why not?

ROCCO: Why not? Because if you go in that room, if you take from Bettina the orange blossoms she wears in her bosom, if you even kiss her, that moment she ceases to be a *mascotte*!

PIPPO: But, hang it all, I love her! She is my wife!

LAURENT: Go in there, you donkey!

8   The lovely "Duet of the Turkeys" can be found on YouTube.

He goes in there. Nine months later, Bettina emerges from her confinement, carrying twins. In her final triumphant aria, she tells the world: "The charm's hereditary!"

* * *

For a time, the human fetish (preferably hunchbacked, dark-skinned, or at least unusually miniature) was evenly matched in American sports with the traditional animal and mineral forms of supernatural aid. "Probably the most popular mascot in America today is the rabbit's foot," noted the Louisville *Courier-Journal* in 1889: "To be a genuine mascot, the foot must be of the left hind leg of a graveyard rabbit caught in the dark of the moon by a cross-eyed colored man who first crawled into the graveyard backwards."

Also efficacious, the paper noted, "is to see a hunchback, or, better still, to get near enough to gently touch his deformity . . . others are firmly convinced that if they can rub the wool on a blind darky's head. . ."

Late that season, a supporter furnished fourteen left-rear rabbits' feet to the Louisville Colonels. The rival St. Louis Browns, however, possessed a more potent weapon, "a homely bull calf which the team dragged around the bases before each game." The Browns won game after game until someone swiped the bovine and they fell to second place behind the Brooklyn Bridegrooms. The Colonels, rabbits' feet and all, finished dead last with 111 losses against 27 victories, one of the worst records in the history of the professional game. Clearly, a more powerful hocus-pocus was required.

"A number of players wear rings they believe possess magic powers," reported the *Washington Post* that same year. "But under no circumstances ever give a ballplayer an opal. They regard the stone as an omen of bad luck."

There were lucky socks and garters, and a first baseman who planted and tenderly nourished a patch of clover near his sack. A pitcher neatly stacked pebbles behind the mound. One man kept a dog with no tail and another made a monkey "his special divinity." Bill Lange of the Chicago White Sox had a famous four-legged chicken: "He will have it lay an egg and cackle for every victory." And Jim Fogarty of the Athletics carried with him a lock of hair, which he obtained "from a dusky maiden in Honolulu." (This last item was of scant use to Fogarty; two years after obtaining it, he died of tuberculosis at age twenty-six.)

The *Syracuse Post-Standard* reported on the anguish of John Day, president of the New York Giants, who tore his hair when informed "that the youngster born with a full beard in Williamsburg had died. Day was sure that he would have in him one of the best mascots in the country."

"San Francisco had a seal in a pool," the eminent sportswriter Hugh Fullerton wrote a few years later. "Years ago, Memphis had a goose that used to stalk solemnly up to the plate to start a rally . . . But hunchbacks and small negroes are considered the luckiest."

* * *

In 1889, a few gentlemen from Chicago, interested in promoting the hurrah! game abroad for patriotic and business reasons, arranged for eighteen star players to tour five continents in four months. Their excursion stopped at the pyramids of Giza, in Colombo, Ceylon, and in Melbourne, Australia, where a local newspaper found the travelers to be "stalwarts every man, lumps of muscle showing beneath their tight fitting jersey garments, and a springiness in every movement which denoted grand animal vigor and the perfection of condition. We could not pick eighteen such men from the ranks of all our cricketers. . ."

Accompanying the stalwarts was "a little son of Ham," an African American named Clarence Duval, one of the game's first celebrity human mascots. According to the *Chicago Times,* Duval, who often frolicked and danced on the sidelines of ballgames in the Windy City, had been spotted in the street and kidnapped by the voyagers, who "contributed to a purse, purchased new clothing for Clarence, and gave him a bath he did not want."

Duval was invited to circumnavigate with the all-stars as their mascot and monkeyshiner, rendering him, in one baseball historian's words, "one of those shadowy figures who decorate historical events but prove elusive in later times." The world tour is both Clarence Duval's pinnacle and his swan song. "The model mascot disappeared from public notice," writes Larry G. Bowman, "and died as the result of injuries he sustained when he was run over by a train in Bloomington, Illinois, in the summer of 1892."

The late 1880s marked the golden age of the African-American charm. In Canada, there was a young man named Willie Hume, "a very small and very fat coloured boy whom the Torontos picked up at Syracuse, [and] travels with them as their Mascotte." The team outfitted Hume in a "gorgeous uniform with gold lamé trimming an inch wide."

"If a little Negro, black as the ace of spades, dwarfed in every limb, and with crossed eyes could have been secured," sniffed the *Topeka State Journal* in 1890, "the ideal mascot would have been presented to the gaze of the base-ball world."

In 1901, a small person of color named L. Marshall Williams, a U.S. Army veteran of the vicious Philippine Insurrection, joined the Philadelphia Phillies as mascot with the moniker of "Lucky." Although barred from sitting in a day coach or sleeping in a Pullman car while traveling across the very republic he had shouldered arms to uphold, Williams joined the club's road trips "on roofs, in the baggage, and other unconventional places."

On July 24, Monte Cross "rubbed the mascot's wool and made two hits, each of which scored a run. Monte will never let that boy go home."

On August 12, Lucky committed an error. The Army veteran was seen wearing a pair of Cross's trousers. "I don't care how much gin and sugar Lucky takes," Monte was reported as saying, "but if he wears my pants, someone might think he was me." Jettisoned by the Phillies, Lucky took up hoodooing on behalf of the Pittsburgh Pirates. He was fired after four days for ineffectiveness, the Bucs having lost three of four in St. Louis.

There were perhaps hundreds more, but the African-American press saw the truth of baseball's racist menagerie. The *New York Age* would comment on yet another sideshow, this one involving a thirteen-year-old boy, as late as the 1930s: "Cecil Haley, New York Giants colored mascot, will know better when he grows older and tries to get a job playing for the same team."

When a waif of color or a hunchback of any hue could not be found, a tiny Caucasian would have to do. When the Detroit Wolverines commenced the 1886 season by winning eighteen home games in a row, three short of the record held by the Chicago White Stockings (which later became the Chicago Cubs, to confusion with the already-existent White Sox), two hundred fans of the Chicagoans entrained for Detroit, each carrying a broom to sweep the challengers away. Leading them was a little blond-haired boy named Willie Hahn. Newspapers reported that the White Stockings' "players and their mascot marched down the platform and placed themselves at the head of the double column of visiting Chicagoans that had formed at the depot, and then with their brooms elevated, the delegation marched out of the depot." Waiting for them at the ballpark were the Wolverines and *their* mascot, "young Charlie Gallagher," a local boy "said to have been born with a full mouth of teeth."

Willie Hahn served three seasons for the South Siders and was replaced a few years later by a three-foot-tall Italian immigrant named Joe Magero, who was spotted selling gum on a street corner and deputized to serve as a "jinx wrecker" for both the White Stockings and their later incarnation as the Cubs. Whatever luck Magero attached to his ball club failed to adhere to the mascot himself. In 1912, "the loyal little rooter" died of pneumonia, aged twenty-one.

The president of the Cincinnati Reds encountered a dwarf nicknamed "Brownie" Burke working as a bellhop in Yellowstone National Park and took him home. Burke provided little in the way of paranormal intervention to the Reds, who finished fourth, fifth, sixth, fourth, and seventh during his tenure with the team.

Like "Lucky" Williams before him, Burke served his country, as well as his baseball club, in uniform. Granted an exemption from the minimum-height standards of the U.S. Army, he shipped out for France with the 90th Infantry Division at the nadir of the War to End all Wars. It was there that he was exposed to German gas canisters, which contributed to the lung disease that led to his death in California in 1931.

In city after city, tragedy was the common coin of human charms. On a beautiful Saturday afternoon in Philadelphia in 1903, the Phillies were tied with the Boston Beaneaters in the fourth inning of the second game of a doubleheader when a noisy commotion began outside the Huntingdon Street Grounds. Maybe it was two raucous drunks, or a young girl hassled by some boys. Fans clustered on an exterior walkway to see what was going on. Dozens of them, and then hundreds crowded the narrow balcony and the structure suddenly gave way, causing "a waterfall of people," "a human avalanche," "an army of boys and men trying to swim in the air" only to land on top of each other in a hecatomb of blood and broken limbs. Twelve of them died.

Mascot Sammy Kelly, eleven years old, had gone home to Gratz Street to rest between games and was on his way back to the ballpark when the wooden trellis crumbled. "As he reached the spot, the body of a falling man struck him," a local paper called *North American* reported. "When the boy was extricated from the writhing heap of humanity on the sidewalk his skull was fractured. He was taken to the Samaritan Hospital in a delirious condition and never regained consciousness."

A pitcher named Bill Duggleby, ace of the woebegone staff, sat by the mascot's cot, day after day.

"Suddenly," the newspapers reported, "[Sammy] opened his eyes and said, 'Shall I open the gate now, Dug?'

"Those were his last words."

Such were the predecessors of Hughie McLoon—the fraternity of the jovial, the mercurial, the taunted, and the damned. The alternatives were much worse. Dr. Wilmer Krusen, Philadelphia's Director of Health and Charities, articulated the popular view that the crippled and deformed were of no use at all:

Club-foot, hunch-back, knock-knee, bow legs, distortion of the shape of the head, tubercular spine, hip-joint disease, and the various other abnormalities of the human framework are defects which can, in most cases, be prevented.

The savages resolved the problem of the physically unfit by allowing nature to determine the survival of the fittest. In this more civilized age, we must resort to more humane, rational, and more effective means of preventing the production of crippled and physically hampered offspring.

Persons who are knowingly affected with disease and thus capable of transmitting hereditary influences, owe it to themselves and to the human race to forgo the right of parentage. And the proportion of deformed children living despite their defects only makes the burden of an increasing human scrap heap more evident.

CHAPTER FIVE

"They Will Last A Lifetime"

I N 1910, HUGHIE MCLOON entered Our Lady of Mount Carmel School on South Third Street, although technically he was no longer a McLoon. In the decennial federal census, he was listed as Hugh Geatens, the "son" of thirty-year-old, Irish-born Peter Geatens of 307 Daly Street, a man whose occupation was recorded as "Junk." Hughie, at age eight, already had three clans (McLoon, Palmer, Geatens), two names, and a half-dozen addresses on his resume.

In the census log, Elizabeth Palmer McLoon, too, had been transformed into a Geatens. Her daughter, Dorothy, was four. Grandmother Mary McLoon was far to the north on West Lehigh Avenue, down the street from the breathtaking new Shibe Park—all brick and steel, an antidote to deadly collapsing plywood balconies—where Connie Mack's White Elephants played. Mary's son Daniel, Hughie's tubercular but true father, had been resting in the Cathedral Cemetery since New Year's Eve, 1907.

To be eight years old in the Greene County Towne in 1910 was to experience violence so raw that it shredded the spirit, and charity so tender that it warmed the soul.

The operators of the city's streetcars had struck in 1909 to force from the Philadelphia Rapid Transit Company higher wages, shorter workdays, and a union with real power. Despite widespread street fighting, they won a raise from twenty-one to twenty-two cents an hour and a reduction to ten hours of work a day, setting an example for seven thousand of the Jewish immigrant women who worked in the city's garment sweatshops, many of them teenagers.

The seamstresses, required to pay for their own thread and needles, laboring in factories whose doors were locked from the outside, abandoned their sewing machines to demand a 10 percent pay raise, a fifty-hour workweek, and the right to form an independent union. As many as three-fourths of them were first-generation Americans, the wretched refuse of the Russian Empire. "How strange and new and shining in this corrupted and weary city" are the faces of the striking alien girls, one society matron noted. "Get the spirit of revolt and become a woman!" the strikers were urged by "the most dangerous woman in America"—the crusader Mary Harris, also known as "Mother Jones."

As the seamstress strike gained momentum, besieged factory owners fought back against "the Girl Army" and threatened to hire African Americans, previously barred from this semi-skilled trade, to take the Hebrews' jobs. Dozens of women, assaulted by management thugs and plainclothes police officers wielding baling hooks, snowballs, tin cans, and bricks, displayed "bruised heads and finger-marked throats."

Although the Girl Army was winning the wider public's sympathy, the Philadelphia *Public Ledger* warned that the ladies "must stop using force and violence" out of fairness to the police, whose "chivalry . . . makes it difficult for them to disperse crowds of female strikers—they are liable to accusations of unmanly cruelty and brutality."

"Gentile girls are in the future to be preferred for the work, as they are better educated and not so stupid as the immigrants," one businessman asserted.

The walkout ended in January 1910: the Girl Army won a fifty-two-and-a-half-hour week and a small increase in wages, and their needles and thread would be furnished by their employers.

But the shirtwaist strike was only the beginning of the city's winter of confrontation and grief. In February 1910, the street-car drivers, aggrieved that their employer had violated the terms of their recent agreement, walked off the job again. Replacement workers were imported from New York. Riots ensued, some joined by thousands.

Dealing with the striking men, police were not straitjacketed by chivalry. At Broad and Spring Garden, "an unidentified man, garbed in working clothes," was "knocked down and trampled upon as the rioters fled from the bluecoats' riot sticks and when the street was cleared he was found lying in the middle of it. He died without regaining consciousness."

"Fresh destruction and bloodshed," said one newspaper, were staining each new snow. There were "more attacks by rioters on trolley cars and blue coats." A girl named Viola Bevan, "struck by a brick during a riot on Thirteenth Street . . . is in a critical condition at St. Joseph's Hospital, where it was stated last night that she could not live many hours longer."

At Sixth and Jackson Streets, one streetcar, with its panicked operator "running at full speed to get away from a mob of riot-ers . . . leaped from the track, smashing headlong into the side of a building, crushing a dozen persons against the wall, killing two and seriously injuring seven others, one of whom may die." Among the victims: "Charles McKenna, 12 years old, of 404 Wolf Street, horribly crushed and instantly killed."

Wolf Street was one short block south of Daly. The street ended directly in front of Our Lady of Mount Carmel. At Ninth and Mifflin, where a new four-story high school was being built in the grand Tudor Revival style, rioters pulled down the half-finished walls and hurled the bricks at the cops. "Mob rule in Philadelphia," screamed the *New York Times*. There were "a score of riots, in which the police and strikers resorted even to shooting." A sixteen-year-old girl was wounded. So was her mother. An eight-year-boy riding in a streetcar surrounded by rioters was hit in the head with a brick; the wound "will result fatally."

The chaos continued until March. The National Guard was called in. The transit company finally began negotiating with its motormen. The drivers held out until April and won a twenty-five-cent hourly wage. Viola Bevan survived the brick and sued the transit company. The suit was dismissed. It was all over in time for opening day

* * *

Connie Mack's baseball Athletics claimed the pennant in two of the American League's first five seasons, but by 1910, after placing fourth, second, sixth, and then second again, the team was clearly in need of supernatural assistance.

Perennially above them in the league tables were the Detroit Tigers, champions in '07, '08, and '09, and led by the indomitable Tyrus Cobb. The "Georgia Peach," whose own mother blasted his father to hell with a double-barreled shotgun, was a snarling, sharp-spiked coil of tenacity, brilliance, and Confederate Lost-Cause resentment: "the most violent, successful, thoroughly maladjusted personality ever to pass across American sports." He was the batting champion of the American League nine years in succession.

Cobb had more than vengeance on his side. To tilt the scales of fortune, he kept as his personal mascot an African-American boy whom he christened "Li'l Rastus," transporting him from game to game in a ventilated steamer trunk that he stashed under his sleeping-car bunk and his hotel bed on road trips through the Jim Crow

League. As star pitcher Christy Mathewson of the New York Giants explained in his ghostwritten 1912 bestseller, *Pitching in a Pinch*, "A great piece of luck is for a ball-player to rub a colored kid's head."

Mathewson, the most idolized player of the nineteen-teens, was no hillbilly but a graduate of Bucknell. "College men are coming into both the leagues, more of them each year, and they are doing their share to make the game better and the class of men higher," he said, "but they fall the hardest for the jinxes." Refuting the *Washington Post*'s contention that the era of superstitious mascot-rubbing was in its final throes, he added: "I don't know as it is anything to be ashamed of at that."

In Mathewson's estimation, the hair of a black boy could not hold a candle to the power of a Louis Van Zelst: "A hunchback is regarded by ball-players as the best luck in the world. If a man can just touch that hump on the way to the plate, he is sure to get a hit, as any observant spectator will notice the Athletics' hitters rubbing the hunchbacked boy before leaving the bench. . ."

The son of a struggling Dutch immigrant cook, Van Zelst, in the summer of 1910, was a fifteen-year-old whose immutable smile belied the torture of a twisted spine. "Thus he has been since birth," reported the *Philadelphia Inquirer*, wrongly. Thus Van Zelst had been only from the age of eight, when he tumbled from a horse-drawn wagon and was crushed and permanently disabled under its rear wheel.[9]

Louis joined the A's late in 1909, bluffing his way into Shibe Park by flashing his smile and brandishing a cigarette-pack trading card portrait of one of the team's outfielders, the popular Reuben "Rube" Oldring. The ticket-taker, "so impressed with the businesslike air of the lad," let him through.

---

9   "Or maybe he was pushed," said Louis's 101-year-old younger brother Theodore, cryptically, in an interview with the author in Philadelphia in 2003. "Maybe he was protecting a friend.")

Connie Mack spotted Louis leaning over the railing and asked him, "How'd you like to tend bats for us today?" Louis, in what the newspaper described as "that quavering, plaintive voice," accepted and the Athletics won, 2–0. Mack invited the boy to come back the next day and to use the Players' Entrance. Only death would part them now.

In 1910, mentored by Oldring himself, Louis Van Zelst—"the poor little bit of nature"—became an intimate and vital part of the Philadelphia A's, to the point of drawing a bi-weekly salary from Mack's closely guarded revenues. The galleries and press box adored him as much as the players did.

"His malformed figure, with the wan, ever-smiling face," impressed "a mental picture thousands have carried from the ball park even after the smoke of battle has ceased to be incense to their nostrils."

"The courageous little hero," the boy "whose organic weakness was such that he could not stand much strenuous travel," a lad "often wracked with pain and bodily torture," with "the courage of a Spartan," who would "don his uniform and suffer a whole afternoon without a whimper or complaint . . . fed the superstition of his comrades with his own body and he did not seem to shrink from making himself a sacrifice in doing this."

"In the misshaped body of Louis Van Zelst," hailed the *Philadelphia Daily News,* had been placed "the soul of a saint and the fortitude of a martyr."[10]

With the martyr in uniform in 1910, something clicked. Rube Oldring batted a career-high .308, the A's became the first American

10   Compare Hugo's Quasimodo of Notre Dame: "With all this deformity, a certain awe-inspiring air of vigor, agility and courage; strange exception to the rule which declares power, as well as beauty, to be the result of harmony.") Hugo, Victor, *The Hunchback of Notre Dame* (New York, Penguin Classics, 1978).

League team to win one hundred games in a season, and they captured the "pennant race," such as it was, leaving the New York Highlanders (later to be called the Yankees) fourteen-and-a-half games behind.

Ty Cobb would wield the bat he called Black Betty for another eighteen seasons with the Tigers, but neither he nor Li'l Rastus ever would win a pennant again.

In the fall of 1910, the Mackmen demolished the redoubtable Chicago Cubs, four games to one in the first World Series win for the A's. With Louis in his road uniform, the A's took two of three at Chicago's North Side Grounds to polish off the Cubs. Twice they clobbered Chicago's pitching ace, Mordecai Peter Centennial Brown, whose own disability was turned to his favor when he discovered that the loss of two digits in a childhood farming accident enabled him to spiral a baseball in a nearly unhittable way. But nobody avowed that deformity made Three Finger Brown some sort of genie.

An unexpected fan of the A's was the fire marshal of Chicago, Jim Horan. "When Chief Horan went to Philadelphia for the World Series," American League president and founder Ban Johnson reported a few weeks later,

> he showed me a perfectly mounted rabbit's foot and said he wanted to give it to Connie Mack. He told me it was the most potent charm and mascot known to the world of superstition. It was the left hind foot of a rabbit which had been caught in the dark of the moon at the edge of an old, deserted cemetery. To make the charm doubly effective and preventive, the man who killed the rabbit was a hunchback. Mack eagerly accepted the gift and took it with him to the Athletics' bench, where he repeated the tale to his players. Chief Bender, who pitched that game, begged for the charm and wore it in his shoe.

Ban Johnson told that story that winter, after returning from the funerals of Marshall Jim Horan and the twenty of his men who died in the fiery collapse of Warehouse 7 of the Chicago Union Stock Yards, just before Christmas in the year of 1910. "Perhaps if Jim Horan has kept that rabbit's foot he might not have lost his life in the stock yards and the A's might have lost," the president said. "I wonder . . . "

The A's themselves had no doubts about the source of their own good fortune. The fifteen-year-old hunchback, Louis Van Zelst, was voted a half-share of the World Series prize money, hard evidence of his role in the team's ascendance. His bounty came to $571, far more than his parents could earn in a year by renting out rooms to students from the University of Pennsylvania, or in their little restaurant, The Dutch Kitchen, on Thirty-third Street.

A photograph from the 1910 Series shows Louis in full uniform and leggings with laced spiked shoes and a cap too big for his head, standing at the lip of the A's dugout, peering keenly out at the field, observant and sage. Behind him, affixed to the bench, just out of focus, sits the forty-eight-year-old Connie Mack, dressed as though for church.

On October 24, 1910, a Baseball Special train from Chicago brought the A's home to Broad Street Station in possession of "the supreme blue ribbon of Fandom," Philadelphia's first World Series championship. The two men who led the procession from the train were the manager and the mascot. "Between the two solid lines of cheering, roaring humanity," Mack and Van Zelst walked together into the victory banquet at the Bellevue-Stratford Hotel. Once again, the streets of a schizophrenic city were given to celebration.

"Away down in their hearts, in that corner where superstition is safely locked up, many of the players felt that the diminutive chap who walked beside the great Connie Mack had a great deal to do with the humbling of the Chicago Cubs," the papers reported.[11]

* * *

When Louis Van Zelst led that parade and basked in his city's sympathy and adoration, eight-year-old Hughie watched from the window of his uncle's office at City Hall.

Each year in those days, the *Philadelphia Inquirer* held its Scholars' Popularity Contest. Readers were invited to fill in a coupon with the name of a student at any school in the city "with pen, pencil, or rubber stamp," to be deposited in special receptacles in every academy in town. Millions of coupons were clipped and entered in 1910 alone.

As first prize, the *Inquirer* offered a gold watch—perhaps not the equal of Rube Waddell's purloined treasure, but if a father were to grab it from his son and pawn it, it might raise enough cash to keep a junkman and his family in groceries for a month, with plenty left over for baseball tickets, a tithe to the church, and beer.

"Animated by friendly rivalry and a keen desire to win one of the beautiful gold timepieces offered to the most popular boys and girls in the public and parochial schools of the city, schoolchildren in every quarter of Philadelphia are devising new ways to add to their already long lists of votes," wrote the *Inquirer.*

> The watches to be given away . . . are solid gold Walthems [*sic*] of standard American make, which are made to retail at $35 apiece . . . They will last a lifetime and be a constant reminder of the energy and popularity of the winners.

11 That Mack, the rigid, dutiful Catholic, actually believed in the intervention of magical children like Louis Van Zelst, and, later Hughie McLoon, was unimaginable to his daughter Ruth, as she said in an interview with the author: "That's a *superstition* and ours is a *religion*," she scolded.

"The ballots will be enumerated carefully, so that no mistake can be made," the promoters vowed, ascribing more probity to a lottery of school kids than to a contest for the United States Senate.

As the Scholars' Popularity Contest entered its home stretch, the *Inquirer* reported that "the race has become closer and the rivalry more keen. The winners in each school are practically assured of having their watches in time for Christmas. These watches will make the handsomest kind of holiday gift for the successful contestants."

When the final coupons were tallied down on South Third Street, a boy named Francis Dieter had turned in 4,351 slips of paper compared to Russell Evans with 3,387; and, far behind them, Joseph Krause with 326.

They were also-rans. A crippled boy on Daly Street had touched the hearts of his immigrant parish in a tumultuous year of championship and carnage, riot and retribution, superstition and suffering. The winner received a staggering 30,090 votes. His name, for the time being, was Hugh Geatens.

CHAPTER SIX

"A Sight For The Gods"

THE GREAT GAME OF baseball can be played without a leg, without an arm, without a voice, without a sound. Strategy is conveyed with the flashing of a finger, or a touch on the brim of a cap. Only the umpire needs to speak at all, and then only in two-word bursts: "Play ball! Strike three! Y'er out!"

Managers kick dirt, make excuses, wave around their fielders, bring in the wrong pitcher at precisely the wrong time. The rest is individual skill and striving. At bat and in the field, raw strength is insufficient, freakish height or bulk a detriment. On the pitcher's mound, rage is inutile, the enemy of control. At the bat, Mighty Casey, his teeth clenched in hate, strikes out. Yet Rube Waddell, drunk and distractible, is in the Hall of Fame, able to master the ball but not himself.

The game cannot be played without precision. It cannot be appreciated without study. And it cannot be won if you are jinxed.

To counteract the whims of fortune, being loony was thought to help. In 1911, the New York Giants placed on the diamond, in full, official uniform, not a hunchback or a child or a Li'l Rastus but a screwball named Charles Victor Faust. This gullible, harmless hulk, a German-speaking prairie farmhand, had been told by a fortune-teller in Wichita, Kansas, that it was his predestination to pitch the New York Giants to a world championship. Soon thereafter, the sooth-sayer promised, Faust would meet and marry a woman named Lulu and together they would raise a fine harvest of sons in a grove of redwood trees as tall as Connie Mack.

Hearing his future scheduled in such detail, Faust hastened to pack a sandwich and some pie (he was inordinately fond of pie), boarded an eastbound train, ambushed the Giants in St. Louis and was granted a "tryout," only to be cruelly spurned when manager John McGraw told him to sprint back to the Planter's Hotel to "pick up his contract" just as the team's train pulled out of the station.

Undaunted, Faust stowed away on a freight car to New York, talked his way into the team's inner sanctum, and clowned and charmed his way into their trust. From then on, with Charles "Victory" Faust on the bench, or in the outfield preparing (in his own mind) to pitch, the Giants won thirty-six games out of thirty-eight, one of the greatest winning stretches in the 150-year history of professional baseball. Immediately, Faust was the cynosure of the half-finished, steel-and-mortar Polo Grounds, which was rising in Upper Manhattan to replace a wooden grandstand consumed by fire on Opening Day. Correspondents found his antics an inex-haustible source of copy. "Mr. Faust has clamped to his shin bones large, flat feet, broad, wide, and splayed, like a fried piece of his native Kansas, and these are all that keep him from taking wing and soaring aloft like a spread eagle as he cavorts over the green-sward reaching for flies that pass thirty feet over his head," read one description.

"He runs like an ice wagon and slides as if he had stepped off a trolley car backward.

He plays ball as if he were a mass of mucilage," reported another.

He was "a human grape-trellis" whose "five-foot legs" were "like deranged calipers and might have snapped right off if not for the anchorage of those Faust feet." He was "the chief comedy attraction." He was "like a garden step ladder suddenly come to life."

He was everywhere: throwing batting practice to the opposition, leading the Catholic Protectory Band, and haranguing team owner John T. Brush for a $10,000 contract, which was $1,000 more than the great Christy Mathewson earned.[12]

But more than mere jollity kept the hick among the players. He left the clubhouse for a week in August to perform on the New York vaudeville stage, mimicking the mannerisms of McGraw and the Giants players, and the team faltered. Another time, he was kidnapped by newspapermen in St. Louis and made to sit on the Cardinals bench. The Cardinals won.

"When he was with us, we won. When he wasn't, we didn't," said the Giants pitcher Richard William "Rube" Marquard, summarizing Faust's contribution in a dozen words.

There were, nevertheless, limits to Faust's alchemy. On September 24, the Giants were defeated in Cincinnati by the sixth-place Reds: a loss, Damon Runyan explained, "that traces back to the breakfast hour and the gross carelessness of the proprietor of the hotel—a man with little regard for the epicure or the idiosyncrasies of genius . . . who ran out of apple pie. This caused the absence from the Giant bench today of Charles Victory Faust . . . Without his apple pie for breakfast, the jinxing power of Charles Victory is wholly nil."

In October, with the National League pennant safely won for the first time since 1905, John McGraw let Faust pitch one real inning

---

12 "On the Giant side," writes E. L. Doctorow in *Ragtime*, "was no midget but a strange skinny man whose uniform was ill-fitting, who had weak eyes that did not align properly and who seemed to shadow the game in a lethargic pantomime of his own solitude, pitching imaginary balls more or less in time with the real pitches. He looked like a dirt eater. . . His name was Charles Victor Faust. He was clearly a fool who, for imagining himself one of the players, was kept on the team roster for their amusement." Doctorow, E.L., *Ragtime* (New York, Modern Library, 1997).

in each of two real games. He struck out none, walked none, and allowed only two hits and two runs. Given the green light by the laughing Boston and Brooklyn opponents, he stole two bases. The fortune-teller had seen it coming: Charlie Faust was a New York Giant.

"Charles Victory Faust of Marion, Kansas, better known as the man who made the Giants famous, has come into his own at last and fulfilled the predictions of the fortune teller who sent him to McGraw," the New York *Herald* wrote. "While he was busy in the outfield yesterday afternoon taking apart a grasshopper to look for the spring that made it jump, McGraw beckoned to him."

The *Herald* went on to claim that Faust cried out "My moment has come!" as he toed the rubber with his "old-fashioned feet, with vital organs in them and flanges on them and mud guards, too."

* * *

In late October 1911, riding the pines again a week after his debut as a major-league pitcher, Victory Faust's skills as a jinx-killer collided with the aura of the A's Louis Van Zelst in one of the most thrilling and portentous series of matches ever waged in any sport. The six World Series games played that rainy fortnight between Connie Mack's Philadelphia A's and John McGraw's New York Giants seemed to occupy a middle-earth between hardball and myth. On one side was enchantment, on the other was lunacy, contesting for the championship of the world.

Forty thousand men and "lady fans" waving flags, their habits adorned with peacock feathers and ostrich plumes, attended every game in the grandest coliseums of their time. The first match in Manhattan was "perhaps the largest attended game that America has ever seen."

"It is a case of sardine packing," according to one report, "nice enough if you are next to your best girl, but perhaps a bit irksome if you have an opposition fan shouting down your left ear and a man with a Chinese gong on your right."

"What a game," according to another. "A sight for the gods!"

For the games at Shibe Park in Philadelphia, the queue extended a full block along West Lehigh Avenue, where nine-year-old Hughie McLoon's grandma and uncle lived, then curled north along Twentieth Street.

Facing John Joseph McGraw, Philadelphia would need all the mania and miracles it could muster. Another hardscrabble Irishman, small and coiled, McGraw sprung from a hamlet called Truxton, New York. He was Connie Mack's ethnic kinsman but his karmic antipode. Terrorized by his father, a traumatized Civil War veteran who had lost four children and a wife to sickness, McGraw grew up to be an irredeemable brawler and umpire-baiter and, in the 1890s, one of the finest third basemen in the National League.

Commanding the squad christened "my big fellows . . . my giants" by an earlier manager circa 1885, McGraw was by 1911 the highest-paid and most illustrious sporting celebrity in New York, earning twice as much in salary as William H. Taft, at less than one-half the president's weight. Over his career, he would return thousands to the league office in fines for punching umpires, libeling officials, cursing opponents, and taunting fans.[13] McGraw would manage in the majors from the Gay Nineties to the Great Depression, winning and being ejected from more games than any National Leaguer of his lifetime.

---

13 "McGraw himself," Doctorow observed in *Ragtime*, "the paternal figure and commander of the team, stood at third base unleashing the most constant and creative string of vile epithets of anyone. His strident caw could be heard throughout the park."

In 1905, McGraw and Mack had met for the first time in a World Series, and in the five games played, the Athletics did not earn a single run. Shut out three times by Christy Mathewson and his "fadeaway" pitch—a protean screwball—the A's disappeared with unseemly haste. They finished a dreadful fourth the following season and continued to wander in the wilderness until 1910, when the cherished Louis Van Zelst changed their fortunes and their faith.

By 1911, Little Van had achieved the full status of icon. When the A's embarked for spring training in San Antonio, the players lined up at North Philadelphia Station for a farewell portrait, and Louis was right in front of Rube Oldring, whose big hands massaged the boy's hump.

"I have just seen the little hunchback," wrote Percy Douglas, 10th Marquess of Queensberry, the English nobleman and playboy engaged by the *Washington Star* to furnish equal measures of fascination and ignorance during the 1911 Series. "I am afraid I am superstitious, and my money goes on Philadelphia. At Monte Carlo, we always try to touch a hunchback before entering the room, and many's the time I have backed and won on thirteen after touching some irate hunchback, whom everyone is trying to pat without his knowing it."

In the second game of the 1911 World Series, the A's third baseman, John Franklin "Home Run" Baker, a Chesapeake ploughman swinging a Bunyanesque, 52-ounce ax, rubbed Louis's hump, "hastily, almost reverently," and hit a sixth-inning, game-winning, two-run home run off the Giants' Rube Marquard (known as the $11,000 Beauty, or the $11,000 Peach, or, after this outing, the $11,000 Lemon). McGraw then turned to Christy Mathewson. As it turned out, he should have used C. Victory instead. In the ninth inning of the third game, Baker detonated another drive over the short right-field wall at the Polo Grounds to tie the score, then singled in the eleventh inning as part of a two-run rally, and the A's beat the unbeatable Mathewson, 3–1.

It downpoured for the next week. When baseball resumed, John McGraw's Giants were beaten men. Reuben Oldring, the A's outfielder who first embraced Little Van in 1909, swatted a three-run homer off the depleted Marquard in game five, despite Marquard's liberal use of tobacco juice to make the ball harder to see on a cloudy day.

In the decisive sixth game, the A's romped, 13–2, and the sainted Louis Van Zelst—"when his agonies were the strongest, his smile was the widest"—was hailed once again as the uncanny source of their timely hitting.[14]

A few weeks later, John Franklin "Frank" Baker's actual war club, "the identical and only bat used by the famous Frank Baker during the World's Series, the bat with which he made the two home runs" was placed on public display on the fourth floor of the Strawbridge & Clothier department store in Center City, Philadelphia. "Louis Van Zelst, Mascot of the Athletics, world's champions, is here, in charge of the bat," an advertisement boasted. "No charge."

By the summer of 1914, Faust had been permanently banished from the Polo Grounds in Manhattan. He followed the sinking sun to Seattle to settle with a brother, only to light out on foot for Oregon, gripped by the delusion of rejoining his teammates, and his mythical Lulu, beneath the mighty redwoods, farther down the coast. In Portland, Faust was accosted and taken to a mental hospital. On the admittance form, he listed his occupation as "professional ball player," which was patently true. Diagnosed with "dementia . . . not improved," he was sent to the asylum at old Fort Steilacoom, Washington. He was thirty-three years old.

---

14 Even before the series ended, Marquard was loudly voicing his suspicion that "Louis Van Zelst, the 'white-haired' hunchback mascot of the Athletics, tipped the Giants' signals off. The boy gets a good view when he goes to pick up the bats, flashes them to the coaches, who give them to the batsman." In 2017 and 2018, the Red Sox and Houston Astros would succeed at the same crime.

Reduced from the roaring thousands of the Polo Grounds to the ministrations of a weary nurse, and far from the immigrant family and the sky-kissed fields from which he burst, Victory Faust was cooped indoors, where his curveball had not the space to bend. He would be dead in less than a year from tuberculosis, or a broken heart.

* * *

On the Fourth of July, 1914, the Boston Braves, managed by the inflammable George Stallings and inspired by a juvenile mascot named Willie Connor, were dead last, fifteen games behind the New York Giants in the National League. Willie Connor was not a hunchback but his eyeglasses were such a curiosity that he was hailed as "the only bat boy in the world who wears spectacles." The intellectualism conveyed by Willie's countenance was so unusual and impressive among the baseballers of the time that the newsmen dubbed him "Mr. Ralph Waldo Emerson Johnnie Baked Beans Connor, a typical Boston highbrow" and designated him the team's "field secretary," rather than its mascot.

Although able-bodied, the field secretary was so motivational that his "Miracle" Braves embarked on a late-summer winning streak and overtook all seven of their rivals, winning their first National League pennant of the twentieth century. They next disposed of Connie Mack, his "$100,000 Infield," and the rest of the Philadelphia A's in four consecutive games to win the 1914 World Series, perhaps the most stunning upset of professional baseball's first half-century.

Willie Connor was lauded for "the careful care of the war clubs with which the Braves humbled the Mack pitching staff." No one in Philadelphia took the defeat harder than Louis Van Zelst. "Perhaps the most poignant grief that Louie ever showed was when his pets, the Mackmen, were routed in that slaughter by the Boston Nationals," it was reported (note that the players were his pets, not the other way around). "Louie always kept a stiff upper lip in defeat, and never shrilled delight in victory. But the tears of disappointment during that series were always close to the surface.

One newspaper story reported that Louie "said but little, but he felt that the Boston series was an Austerlitz if not a Waterloo to him as a mascot." Alas, this was true. Little Van's pets would not win another league pennant in his lifetime, and he would never tend their bats again.

As the Pennsylvania winter ended in 1915 and the Athletics boarded the steamship *Apache* for the long voyage to Jacksonville, Florida, Little Van was not with them. Whether still shaken by the World Series sweep, or bilious at the prospect of three days at sea, he remained home and lent his angelic aura to the University of Pennsylvania varsity while awaiting the Athletics' return.

On Tuesday, March 16, "he went to Franklin Field and was hailed with delight by the students. On Wednesday, St. Patrick's Day, he became very ill. From that time he was unable to leave his bed and on Thursday night he learned that he could not live."

A few hours later, "a crumpled, pain-wracked little body that tossed and writhed in agony got relief," and Louis Van Zelst, "known and beloved of all the baseball world," "the most envied boy in the country," now, at twenty, nearly a man, was dead. Philadelphia papers reported the scene at his deathbed:

"The smiling little hunchback had prayed to die."

"The pain was unbearable and he prayed and prayed to die."

"Dry-eyed, his parents stood around him in the little bedroom and spoke words of encouragement to him—tried to alleviate his misery."

"And with his last words he thanked them and asked them not to be sorry—that he was glad to die."

"He is gone away," wrote Harry Keck in the *Pittsburg* (not yet spelled Pittsburgh) *Daily Post,* "where no team will ever defeat his 'pals.'"

The cause of death was paralysis of the spine from that long-ago fall from the wagon, or Bright's Disease, or "a complication of diseases," or the Miracle Braves.

In the Philadelphia *Press,* on March 22, 1915, with Louis Van Zelst newly inhumed at Holy Cross Cemetery, east of the city that adored him, a man named Richard J. Beamish wrote a poem entitled "The Mascot's Death."

It began:

> I can close my eyes and see you now, an Elfin dauntless shape,
> As you squatted in holes you had dug for luck while the home crowd hung agape.

It ended:

> I saw you again as the crowd poured out, and your face was white with pain.
> Your hour had passed, and your little frame was upon the rack again.
> "You pulled them through, you Louie," I said, and you raised a visage grave.
> "I did my best," you answered low, and I marked the smile so brave. . .

A few days later, the headlines read, "Athletics Won't Have Mascot in Hunchback's Place." The hole left by Little Van, said Connie Mack, was too hard to fill. The Athletics would have to "worry along the coming season without a mascot and thus disappoint thousands of juvenile rooters who have sought the proud position."

However, there was another ball club in residence on Lehigh Avenue. The National League Phillies, overshadowed by the six-time American League champion White Elephants down the block, had customarily finished sixth or seventh since the Mackmen rose to prominence in 1902.

They needed a hunchback of their own, and they found one in a boy named Raoul Naughton, aged seventeen, in 1915.

"Some little boys grow up with the idea of ultimately becoming President," noted the Philadelphia *Evening Public Ledger,* introducing Raoul. "Others, objecting to the age limitation put on this desirable job, decide not to wait and dream dreams of one far more precious, that is to say, becoming the mascot of a big league baseball team."

Naughton was not paid for his labors, but this was not an obstacle. "If I had the money and they would take it," he said, "I'd be willing to pay to be the mascot of a team like the Phillies."

For most of the 1915 season, there was no other team like the Phillies, at least in the National League. They romped home in first place, their last pennant until 1950. In the first game of the World Series, the Phils rubbed batboy Naughton's hump to the tune of a 3–1 victory over the Boston Red Sox. But then, Boston's pitching took control, and the Beaneaters won the next four. Exit Raoul.

CHAPTER SEVEN

"Death To The Demon"

AFTER A DECADE OF excommunicable cohabitation and already sharing a surname on the United States Census, Peter and Elizabeth Geatens were finally, formally married on January 19, 1915, for reasons known only to themselves. The Commonwealth of Pennsylvania, on its marriage form, asked if the groom was "an imbecile, epileptic, of unsound mind, or under guardianship of a person of unsound mind, or under the influence of any intoxicating liquor or narcotic drug?"

Also, "Is applicant afflicted with any transmissible disease?" And, "Has applicant within five years been an inmate of any county asylum or home for indigent persons?

To these questions, the applicants marked "No."

"Occupation of applicant's father?"

Dead.

"Mother?"

Dead.

"Is the applicant physically able to support a family?"

"Yes," wrote Peter Geatens, who upgraded his occupation from "Junk" to "Dealer." He was still bunking at 307 Daly Street. His affianced, not too shy to give the same address, declared herself to be both a widow named Elizabeth McLoon and a bride who had "never been married before."

The papers were duly stamped by the Orphans' Court of Philadelphia County and everybody went home to the slum to celebrate. Two years later, the never-married widow would be pregnant with a boy that she and Peter would christen Daniel, the same given name as the now-deceased clerk Daniel McLoon whom Elizabeth wedded in 1901.[15]

* * *

In the same week that Elizabeth McLoon and Peter Geatens finally wed, a former major-league outfielder was back in Philadelphia, where he played thirty-one games for the Phillies in 1890 at the end of his professional career. A fleet base runner but a weak hitter, William Ashley Sunday was not in town for baseball or to toast the newlyweds at 307 Daly. Sunday's mission was the immediate, total, permanent eradication of brewed, distilled, and fermented beverages from American life, a struggle consuming his own once-tinctured soul and cleaving the social fabric of a dipsomaniacal nation. In 1915, Billy Sunday was the most famous and perfervid professional Christian outside the Holy See.

In the dozen years since a property owner on East Girard Avenue refused to sell his premises to the hotelier Hugh P. McLoon lest it be used for the provision of intoxicating liquor, the temperance movement had scored occasional victories: a scattering of statewide bans in New England, the Deep South, and elsewhere, and the banning of booze aboard U.S. Navy vessels in 1913. But its ultimate goal

15 The child Daniel would grow up to become the gentleman wont to bludgeon his son and daughter with a knot of wood if they were slow in mixing his drink, his name a constant reminder to his older stepbrother Hughie of the father he lost before he ever knew him.

of national, Constitutional, enforceable, perpetual Prohibition remained unfulfilled.

Following the death of the ax-wielding Carry (or Carrie) Nation four years earlier, the flamboyant Billy Sunday had led the crusade for total illegalization. He specialized in conflating what could be a secular, scientific call for sobriety in the name of public health with a tent-revivalist's blazing Biblical certainties.

In his four decades of continuous campaigning, starting in the 1880s, it is estimated that one hundred million people walked a mile or straddled a horse or hopped a trolley to hear Billy Sunday sing to them of Jesus and bedevil them about gin. His quest began while he was still an active ballplayer, when, as if in a scene from *Guys and Dolls,* the hymns wafting from a Windy City sidewalk ministry inspired him to abandon alcohol forever. Still preaching the week he died, no other Christian orator of the pre-broadcast era would project his personal propaganda so effectively and so entertainingly into as many human ears as Billy Sunday.

Born the same year as his fellow teetotaler Connie Mack (they played against each other for four seasons), Sunday's grievances were manifold: the Pabsts and Busches and Blatzes who soaked the continent in foamy brew; the "wet" legislators who stymied the enactment of a nationwide ban on booze—politicians, he trumpeted, who were "low-browed, hog-jowled, strength-sapping, whisky-soaked."

"I will fight them till hell freezes over," he vowed. "Then I'll buy a pair of skates and fight them on the ice."

Beginning in January 1915, in a temporary timber tabernacle on the newly carved-out Ben Franklin Parkway, Sunday preached once or twice a day before crowds of ten and twenty thousand at a time, "standing on one foot, his fist high over his head, his eyes flaming fire, and the perspiration streaming down his face."

"I know what your dirty, crooked, sinning, lawless booze gangsters have done," Sunday thundered in Philadelphia. "But I don't give a rap what you do. I fight you to the last ditch. You don't frighten me!"

Alcohol was so addictive, Sunday railed, that "no man can stop lapping up the stuff by his own will power." He must turn to Christ, "for a man might bear the scars caused by the devil being in him in the shape of whisky, but it would be death to the demon if the man keep the Lord in his heart."

Billy Sunday's shouting, his fist-pumping, his leaping onto the lectern like an oracle possessed, left the thousands on the benches transfixed and terrified: "America needs a tidal wave of the old-time religion . . . America needs to be taken down to God's bathhouse and the hose turned on her, and the time isn't far distant when the wheels of God's judgment are going to go sweeping through this old God-hating world, and I want this audience to join me in a pledge that you will never rest until this old God-hating, Christ-hating, whiskey-soaked, Sabbath-breaking, blaspheming, infidel, bootleg-ging old world is bound to the cross of Jesus Christ by the golden chains of love!"

"The hospital had plenty to do during the service yesterday," the Philadelphia *Evening Public Ledger* reported in January 1915. "Dr. W. H. Shane, the superintendent, treated ten persons who had fainted in the audience. One of these, in the evening, was a man who had gone to the tabernacle with a half-jag. When Dr. Shane brought him to his senses, he said: 'Boss, I'm through with that stuff. After what I've heard about it tonight, and being knocked out and letting it make a fool of me before this throng, I don't ever intend to hit it again.'"

Some mornings, Sunday left his tabernacle and the common, thirsty Philadelphians and took his soberer-than-thou harangue directly to the parlors of the Drexel Biddles, the Harrison Smiths, the Van Valkenburgs, "hurling shafts of fire at sin's shame." The rich, he warned them, are "priests of gold making money by the bucket-ful, but going to hell in carload lots."

In 1920, the United States Constitution will make it a crime to raise a cheering cup at the end of a week of toil, or on the Fourth of July, or at a virgin widow's wedding.

* * *

Alcohol, the essential oil of urban conviviality, the balm of rural isolation and industrial drudgery, had been an integral part of baseball since the very first inning. "Baseball is the National Pastime. Beer is the National Drink," summarized Ty Cobb in a 1909 newspaper advertisement for a brew called Becker's Best.

Every day for seven or eight months, when his sunlit labors were over, a ballplayer was left to his leisure in a metropolis that adored him, or in another city far from parents, wives, and pastors, with plenty of spending money, nothing to do until three the next afternoon, and nowhere to go save a midnight depot or the airless cell he shared with a stinking, snoring outfielder. The result, too often, or perhaps less often than one might imagine, was plenty of time for consorting with gamblers and impermanent girlfriends, and indulging a fondness for the national drink.

Baseball history revels in the drunken exploits of long ago. Some tales are cautionary: for instance, the case of Rube Waddell. Or that of Charlie Sweeney, a right-handed pitcher for the Providence Grays in the 1880s whose manager sent his first baseman and captain, a player named Old Reliable Start, to the box (there was no mound yet) to remove Charlie from a game:

> He asked Sweeney to go out in the field. Sweeney was drunk, but I didn't know it. Start's request made Sweeney mad. He didn't take it in the way it was meant. He walked off the field. I went after him, but couldn't get him to come back.
>
> He called me a vile name. The president of the club went to

him and asked him what he meant, and he called him every-thing vile on the calendar. Sweeney was very drunk.

Ten years later, in a San Francisco saloon, an elegantly wasted Charlie Sweeney shot a man during an argument, then blacked out. Informed the next morning of his victim's death, Sweeney "broke down and wept bitterly." He served one-third of a ten-year prison stretch, contracted tuberculosis, and died two weeks before Opening Day 1902.

Then there was the horrendous saga of Ed Delahanty, who in 1903 was the star right fielder of the Washington Senators, a lifetime .346 hitter, one of five brothers to reach the majors and, as described in his obituary in the *New York Times,* "a roughneck at heart" who had "that wide-eyed, half-smiling, ready-for-anything look that is characteristic of a certain kind of Irishman. He had a towering impatience, too, and a taste for liquor and excitement."

Riding east across Ontario from a game in Detroit one night in a sleeper of the Michigan Central Railway, Delahanty, who "had five drinks of whiskey," brandished a straight-razor, tried to yank a woman out of her berth by her feet, "and became so obstreperous" that the conductor "had to put him off the train at the Canadian end of the Niagara Falls bridge":

> After the train had disappeared across the bridge, Delahanty started to walk across, which is against the rules. The night watchman attempted to stop him, but Delahanty pushed the man to one side. The draw of the bridge had been opened for a boat, and the player plunged into the dark waters of the Niagara.

The great slugger's body was found the next day in the churning stream, minus a leg sheared off by the propeller of the *Maid of the Mist.*

Occasionally, the monopsonists who entrusted to themselves the sport's civilization attempted to cleanse their realm of gamblers, game-throwers, and hopeless drunks. In 1881, the National League blacklisted ten men for "confirmed dissipation," losing on purpose, and other sins. Among them was the catcher, strongman, and inveterate drinker Lew "The Hoss" Brown, who would be exiled from the diamond more than once for alcoholism. During one of his suspensions, Brown, who was so talented and unmanageable that he bounced around eight teams in nine seasons in three major leagues, found work serving lager in a Boston whorehouse. He also moonlighted in stage performances of *As You Like It* as the grappler Charles: "I wrestle for my credit; and he that escapes me without some broken limb shall acquit him well."

One night in January 1889, Brown slammed his knee into a stone cuspidor while playfully tussling with a customer. (In other accounts, The Hoss's boss-lady whacked him with a gas pipe).

As Billy Sunday might have warned, the wages of suds were death. Brown's wound became infected, the leg had to be amputated, he got pneumonia and died.

* * *

By 1915, Billy Sunday had acquired some staunch allies from his old profession in his quest for the abolishment of liquor. The prelate of the public teetotalers was Connie Mack. Two-hundred-proof abstemious in his personal life, the practical Mack lobbied for decades, unsuccessfully, to have beer sold in the stands at his ballpark. He also permitted his men a post-game brew or two in the clubhouse. And at home games, writes Bruce Kuklick in *To Every Thing a Season*, "relief pitchers would leave the right field gate near the bullpen to tilt a few during the early innings of games in which the Phillies piled up a big lead."[16] But after sixty-six years of big-league ball, Mack could still recite word-for-word his promise to his mother that he would never touch alcohol if permitted to sign up with a professional team.

Mack also vouchsafed that "not one man of the '$100,000 Infield' had ever touched a drop of liquor." The most self-righteous member of the infield quartet was Eddie Collins, the second baseman and a graduate of Columbia University. Later on, speaking on a sabbath morning in 1916 to five hundred parishioners at a church in Palmyra, New Jersey, Collins "handed booze some wallops that would have done credit to Billy Sunday," according to the *Philadelphia Inquirer.*

"I come to bring a message to your young people, from a baseball player's viewpoint, of the necessity of clean living and I will be glad if anything I say will help any of you fight the battle of life," the future Hall of Famer testified. "Temperate living is necessary for success in any field of action."

"No quartet of arrows ever flew straighter," agreed Connie Mack biographer Norman Macht of Collins, third baseman Franklin "Home Run" Baker, shortstop Jack Barry and first-sacker John Phalen "Stuffy" McInnis. But within months, $75,000 worth of them would be off to greener pastures.

For more than a century, baseball historians have tried to divine how and why the mighty Philadelphia Athletics, after winning four American League pennants and three World Series in five seasons, so completely and irretrievably collapsed in the space of a few short weeks, and why the Mack decided to unload so many of his stars in such short order; a fatal housecleaning that is still seen as either shrewd business or abject surrender.

16 Kuklick, Bruce, *To Everything A Season* (New Haven, Princeton University Press, 1993).

"The myth persists that because of the loss of the 1914 World Series, Connie Mack immediately took an axe and gave his roster forty whacks," writes Macht, a former minor-league executive who devoted more than twenty years to his monumental three-volume biography of a man whom he met only once in person, when Mack was eighty-five.[17] Macht contends the implosion occurred gradually, the cumulative result of an aging roster, disharmony, the retirement of Home Run Baker, and the arrival of a Baltimore saloonkeeper's incorrigible son named George Herman Ruth to the roster of the rising Boston Red Sox.

In 1914, barely a dozen years after the formation of the American League, a third circuit called the Federal League once again tantalized indentured players with the chance to earn carload lots of money for the same two-hour workday. The new league's franchises were flung from Missouri to Newark to Buffalo (but not to Philadelphia). Their owners spent like madmen. Their upstart league would fail in a hundred weeks, but not before doing damage to Shibe Park.

Weeks after their shocking four-game annihilation by the Braves in the World Series, two of Mack's best pitchers left for the Feds. Then the Chicago White Sox offered fifty thousand dollars for Collins, and Mack accepted and reclaimed from Cleveland the thirty-nine-year-old, overweight Napoleon Lajoie, one of the paramount stars of the century's first decades, to replace the temperate collegian.

The cataclysm accelerated. With Home Run Baker obstinately preferring his cornfield to the infield, Mack tried ten different third basemen in the span of a few awful weeks at the start of the 1915

---

17 Macht, Norman L. & Connie Mack III, *Connie Mack and the Early Years of Baseball* (Lincoln, University of Nebraska Press, 2007); Macht, Norman L., *Connie Mack: The Turblent and Triumphant Years, 1915-1931* (Lincoln, University of Nebraska Press, 2012); Macht, Norman L., *The Grand Old Man of Baseball: Connie Mack in his Final Years, 1932-1956* (Lincoln, University of Nebraska Press, 2015).

season, with no success. Two of the dynasty's three regular outfielders were let go. Shortstop Barry headed to the Bosox for one-fifth of what Chicago paid for Collins.

"My team is somewhat demoralized by this," Mack admitted. "But I resent the accusation that my team is the worst club on earth."

He spoke too soon. On the seventh of May, 1915, when the German submarine *U-20* destroyed the British liner *Lusitania* with 139 citizens of the neutral American republic on board, the Athletics were in seventh place and falling, on their way to becoming the only major-league club of the twentieth century to plummet from first to eighth in a single year. Sober, honest, devout, desperate Connie Mack, his dynasty crumbling, his grandstand vacant, his heroes scattered, his magic touchstone gone, needed to find a new protector against strikeouts, jinx, and ruin.

On May 11, Woodrow Wilson, two years into his presidency, spoke at Convention Hall. He had been silent since the sinking, studiously formulating "a new ideal of Americanism" that "evolved from the silent and solitary reflection of the President after hours of study in the White House." Now he attempted to turn the nation's gaze away from anger, and toward "faith, patience and charity."

"There is such a thing as a man being too proud to fight," the president said before an audience of thirty thousand Philadelphians, including two thousand newly sworn citizens and more than a thousand security men in uniform and mufti:

> There is such a thing as a nation being so right that it does not need to convince others by force that it is right.
> Think first of humanity.
> America was created to unite mankind.

* * *

On the very same day the *Lusitania* sank, a man named Colonel Charles Keegan launched a lawsuit against the dry and pious Billy Sunday, claiming that the prohibitionist had left his house at 1914 Spring Garden Street in ruins while staying there during his two months in Philadelphia.

"Furniture was smashed, walls gouged, china broken," said a newspaper report on the $3,034.75 suit:

> There were six doors off their hinges. A five-foot jardinière in the front room was broken and patched together again. Someone broke the leg off a heavy leather armchair in Billy Sunday's room. The piano stool was smashed.
>
> A good many things were missing. Among these is a marble dog which graced the Keegan reception room, the big toe of a statue of a girl; a silver-plated syrup jug and a quantity of clothing.
>
> Colonel Keegan refused to confirm a report that several bottles of gin and whisky he had left in a padlocked trunk room were empty and the lock missing when he took possession again.

The fire-breathing Sunday had moved on to Paterson, New Jersey, with his wife, known as "Ma." A pair of correspondents from the *Evening Public Ledger* followed them and climbed onto the running board of Ma's automobile to ask about the house on Spring Garden and, specifically, the missing liquor and the two dozen whisky glasses and thirty-eight beer mugs that had disappeared from the Colonel's cabinets.

> "What do you mean?" she called, doubling her fists. "What do you mean standing here asking me such things? Oh, I'll punch in your face!"

Mrs. Sunday swung at the reporter, missed him, and hit the chauffeur.

"Hang the people in Philadelphia who think we drink a gallon a day."

"Drive on," she called.

CHAPTER EIGHT

"Valet Of The Willows"

T HE GRAND ENTRANCE OF Shibe Park that towered over
the tremulous Hughie McLoon on the morning of Tuesday,
July 11, 1916, was "an expression of culture, taste, and man-
ners," a pretentious yet appropriate basilica of "rusticated bases,
composite columns, arched windows and vaultings, and a domed
tower . . . the massive front had Ionic pilasters flanking recessed
arches on either side of the building." A terra-cotta statue of the
spindly, saintly Connie Mack, and another of Benjamin Franklin
Shibe, the great arena's aspirational builder, stood guard above the
French Renaissance doors, as if at Notre-Dame. The brickwork
exuded permanence, the statuary oozed hubris, and the game within
the gates offered the very essence of Americanism to the newest
residents of the city.

The landslide winner of the 1910 Scholars' Popularity Contest
tiptoed inside. A few years later, he would explain what happened
next to the Philadelphia *Evening Public Ledger*: "I us'ta go to the ballpark every day an' watch the A's play. One day I went there and saw
a big guy hittin' them out from the plate. I asked 'im about gettin'
the job as mascot, and he told me he would do what he could and
told me to see Connie Mack."

This would require of Hughie not only a deep breath and a gulp of confidence but a climb of two flights of stairs to Mack's three-room suite, "done in an equally opulent manner and later known as the oval office." There, in a living museum of framed photographs, alabaster white elephants, and a bench made from baseball bats, was Mack himself.

I went up the steps to Connie's office and couldn't open the door. A big fellow saw me tryin' and pulled it wide for me. "Hey, Connie," he shouted, "There's a big pitcher for you from the West." I felt queer, and they all began to laugh and kid me, but I stood there and told Mister Mack what I wanted, anyhow.

He told me that the team had been losing a bunch of games—I think it was eighteen straight—and if they won the first day I was on the job they would keep me. I tol' him I'd bring him luck, and I did. The A's won 'at day, and I stayed.

Mister Mack used to tell me it wasn't me bringin' 'em bad luck, but he was developing ball players, and would some time get another pennant winner. I think he will, too.

Oh, yeh. The big man hittin' em out was Lajoie.

* * *

July 11, 1916, was a perfect day for a doubleheader but the A's were a safe bet to lose both ends. All of the woes that befell the 1915 Athletics—Mack's sell-off of his pennant-winning veterans; the loss of his pitching aces to the Federal League; the raw rookies; the batters who couldn't hit; the dive to the American League cellar; the glum, depleted fan base; four errors in a single game by the once-imperial Lajoie—had gotten even worse the following season.

By the third week of the 1916 campaign, the A's had lost ten of their first thirteen games. They were snug in the league basement, and pessimists were calling them the Pathetics. But they were just getting warmed up.

John Phalen McInnis—"that's the stuff!" they used to cheer him—still was a stalwart at first base, but Stuffy was anchoring a $10 infield. Grantland Rice, writing for the New York *Tribune*, limned him as the "last of the Mohicans":

> Piking along with the trailers,
> Here as the summer flits,
> Sometimes isn't it lonesome
> Wasting your two-base hits?
> Batting above Three Hundred
> While Hanging on to a dream
> Swept from the years behind you
> Last of the old Regime

The team that the successor regime force-marched onto the field every day was green as the outfield grass. Mack would allow almost anyone a tryout. Four catchers were mustered: the first receiver got typhoid fever on the boat to spring training; the second split his hand open on the first day of practice; the third doubled over with appendicitis; the fourth ran into a wall chasing a fly ball, broke his jaw, and was knocked unconscious. At one point in the season, five of Mack's players hailed a line drive from Shibe Park. (By autumn, fifty-one adults and juveniles would play at least one game on the roster of a team that required only nine at a time. For a dozen of those, one afternoon would encompass the entirety of their major-league career.)

"The season of 1916 is going to be experimental," shrugged Mack. Some of the rookies were so useless that Mack made them shower with the umpires. From the grandstand, "That's the stuff!" was replaced with "That's the stiff!"

The incompetence was sensational. One outing in May, three Philadelphia pitchers combined to walk eighteen Detroit Tigers. The next day, they walked eleven Tigers. The next day, ten more, then another ten. Watching this sad defile from the outfield, the next-to-last Mohican, Rube Oldring, quit the team.

Even as the A's foundered, Mack never stopped scouring the nation, and especially its college campuses, for fresh talent. He also ordered his groundskeepers to allow the grass to rise to a height of three or four inches, the better to slow the visiting team's hits before his demoralized infielders could fumble them.

In July, the Cleveland Indians sent a telegram to American League headquarters to protest Shibe Park's Amazonian shag. It hardly mattered. The A's baby shortstop, Whitey Witt made three errors and Cleveland won, 12–5.

On a visit to Boston's Fenway Park, Witt was honored before a game by fans from his Massachusetts hometown. Presented with a gold watch and "sundry other tokens of esteem," Witt was so bedazzled that, when he came to bat, he steamed into third base with a soaring triple, only to be called out for "neglecting to touch the first cushion en route."

"Rankest gloom in camp of Mackmen," headlined the *Sporting News*. Correspondent William Weart blamed the A's downfall on the fact that Mack's collegians actually went to college. "Too Much Exams Put Them to the Bad Physically," the headline read. All of the players were "either actually ill, or out of condition, caused by the fact that they had been compelled to forget baseball for a time and take their examinations. . ."

Connie Mack tried to be philosophical—"You can't win them all"—but the losing hurt. According to Norman Macht, one daughter would recall that "when Dad would come home after a game, Mother would always go upstairs and put a shot of whiskey on top of his chest of drawers, and she would no sooner go back down than he would take it into the bathroom I used and dump it in the sink. She was probably right that it was good for him. But he didn't want it."

By the time of Hughie's tryout, the A's had won eighteen games and lost fifty-three. The St. Louis Browns were in town, wallowing in seventh place yet eleven games in front of the Pathetics, who had dropped nine straight. July 11 promised two stink-outs for the price of one, even with a little gap-toothed boy in a pinstripe shirt, two weeks shy of his fourteenth birthday, along the baseline.

The first slugger to take a bat from Hughie McLoon on his inaugural day as a major-league mascot was the second baseman and leadoff hitter Otis Carroll Lawry, age twenty-two. He had been with the team for two weeks, not much longer than the batboy, after finishing his semester at the University of Maine. Touted by Mack as "the next Eddie Collins," Lawry had played in seven previous big-league contests and had yet to taste victory. The A's were already behind, 2–0 in the bottom of the first, when he accepted his war club from the novice lucky charm and strode to the plate.

Lawry went 0-for-5. The A's fell behind, 8–0, after four innings. They scored three in the bottom of the sixth to make a comeback appear at least theoretical, then meekly made their exit, taking with them Hughie's first of two chances to wreak some magic and keep the job that was every boy's dream.[18]

"Putrid pitching by two recruits and the general all-around inefficiency of the Athletic squad lost the opening brawl," wrote the

18 The A's starting pitcher in the opener, a twenty-one-year-old local kid and Penn State matriculant named George Hesselbacher, lasted three innings. He started again the next day, lasted one inning, and was dismissed by Mack a week later, never to appear in a big-league game again. The Browns' left fielder, who doubled off Hesselbacher to lead off the game, was Burt Shotton from Brownhelm, Ohio. One lifetime and two world wars later, in 1947, the same Shotton would manage the Brooklyn Dodgers, calmly guiding Jackie Robinson, the modern game's first African-American player, through his rookie season, while Connie Mack still was running the A's at the age of eighty-five.

pseudonymous Jim Nasium of the *Philadelphia Inquirer*. "The less said about the first fuss, the better."

The next Eddie Collins was benched for the second match of the doubleheader. Mack's starting pitcher was a Minnesotan named Leslie Ambrose Bush, a hard thrower known as "Bullet Joe," who hadn't won since the first of June. In the first inning Jimmy Walsh led off with a base on balls. Craftily, the A's turned a couple of walks, a couple of singles, and a bunt into a 2–0 lead. Bullet Joe needed nothing more. Scattering five singles, he shut out the St. Louis Browns, 3–0. Hughie McLoon's magic powers were proved, his job preserved. The town went wild.

MACK'S MIDGET MASCOT MAY
PUT KIBOSH ON THE JINX
Hughie McLoon, 58 pounds, now on
the job as Official Valet of
the Willows
Another little hunchback

The ghost that hovers over Shibe Park, not the one that struts when the Mack help collect their hard-earned lucre, but the one that jinxes the Athletics; the one that made them lose sixty games until yesterday—may be banished with the completeness of the snakes from the Emerald Isle.

While the Mack sand lot sleuths were sherlockholmsing in the four corners of the land of the free, Connie himself seemed to be overlooking a bet. What he needed was a mascot. Whenever a mascot's not on the alert, you can be sure a jinx will be on the job, and as the Mack school had none, why the jinx pitched its tent there for a long stay.

But today there's another story. Mack has a mascot on the job. He is Hughie McLoon and he weighs fifty-eight pounds.

Hughie is fourteen years old and lives as 2546 West Lehigh Ave. He is a student at the Mt. Carmel School.

He hopes to break the long streak of bad luck that has haunted Shibe Park so long that the players expect to see a shark drop out of the spigot in the shower baths.

The little mascot said yesterday: "I am certainly glad Mr. Mack picked me for the job. I always liked to play base ball but I am a very little fellow and never had much chance. I don't know how much luck I will bring but I am going to listen to all the players and take care of their bats the best I know how.

"The people in the stands don't know it, but every player's bat has to be in a certain spot so that when that player comes to bat he can find his club without any trouble. Players are particular about their bats."

He succeeds Louis Van Zelt [*sic*] who died two years ago.

Inspired by their victory, a laughingstock no longer, the Philadelphia Athletics rushed right out and won one game of their next twenty-nine.

* * *

One detail went unremarked in the giddy press on July 11. At Shibe Park, the new batboy told Connie Mack and the *Bulletin* that his surname was McLoon. But at Our Lady of Mount Carmel School, and on the United States Census for 307 Daly Street, he still was a Geatens. As he turned fourteen, Hughie was one boy with two names, two homes, and two families. "It's easy," he said of his new career with the A's. "All yuh gotta do is hang around, keep the bats in a straight row and never get 'em crossed or crooked if yuh like the job much, and help the players whenever yuh get a chance.

"It's hard at first, then it's easy.

"Funny, huh?"

CHAPTER NINE

"Kiss The Flag"

DESPITE THEIR BACCALAUREATES and their grand old manager, the 1916 Philadelphia A's were so outclassed, so lamentably, ludicrously unsuccessful day after day that, at one point near the end of the season, every other team in the American League boasted a winning record thanks to a summer of feasting on the White Elephants. United in ridicule, the nation piled on. "Oh Jack, it's in the paper," wailed Florrie Keefe, anguished wife of Jack Keefe, the fictional hurler of Ring Lardner's epistolary *You Know Me Al* stories of the nineteen-teens. "They have traded you to Philadelphia."[19]

"Well, for a minute" wrote Jack, who was not among the league leaders in spelling, "I felt kind of stuned and then I snatched the paper out of her hand and read it over and over again and finely I got it through my head that it was true and Florrie was still snuffleing and I guess maybe I snuffled a little too."

In real life, Lardner was no less savage with the A's: "It looks kind of improbable for them to win the pennant now unless the season is extended a couple of years."

---

19 Lardner Jr., Ring, *You Know Me Al: A Busher's Letters* (Mineola, Dover Publications, 2016).

A fan wrote to the Philadelphia *Evening Public Ledger* in protest of the belittling: "What kind of sportsmanship is it in panning the Athletics day after day? Everyone realizes that the team is not good now, but the fans and public are indulgent enough to wait until Connie builds up another machine, especially as the town has already been glutted by him with world beaters. It comes with particularly bad grace to pan the A's in Philadelphia." A comic strip in the same paper fired right back.

"Haven't the Athe-letics been scandiliferously back-ward this year?" jested a stick figure named Harum.

"O my yes!" gasped his friend Scarum. "But! They can still go to the front."

"How?"

"By joining the army!"

This was not a jest that any American would be giggling at nine months later. But in the American summer of 1916, the Somme was worlds away. The hearty crew of the *Deutschland* was being banqueted in Baltimore. By season's end, as Woodrow Wilson and Charles Evans Hughes rumbled toward a November vote, the Washington Senators were glued to seventh place in the American League, fourteen games behind the champion Red Sox. The Philadelphia Athletics were staggering home forty games behind Washington.

Unlike the field-tested, pennant-winning, jinx-busting hocus-pocus of Louis Van Zelst and Raoul Naughton, the engagement of Hughie McLoon in midseason brought no sudden uplift to the Athletics. If such a thing were possible, the team actually got worse after he joined. Still, he exulted. He was fourteen years old, and the game and the heroes and the stadium and the long, sunlit grass were his.

"Some of 'em want yuh ta' give 'em the bat with thuh handle t'wards the dugout," said Hughie, explaining his duties, "an' others want the big end pointed that ways, an' still others want 'a pick up their own—it's funny."

"He is firm, fearless, and at times defiant in his beliefs," sportswriter Wallace McCurley said of the boy. "Certainly he is unchangeable. . ."

Hughie has the greatest admiration for Mr. Mack and calls him the greatest manager—bar none—that ever came down the pike.

"He's tried out some horrible bums an' never let 'em know they really was rotten," Hughie said. "Funny, huh?

"Awh, it's not so bad," he said. "All yuh have to do is get in right with the players. They're all good guys and treat yuh right after yuh know what to do and when to do it.

"Why, would yuh believe it, one of those birds used to make me hand him two bats at once, and if anybody but me took it in their hands he 'ud throw it away and get out a new one.

"'At was Stuffy McInnis. Funny, huh?

"Stuffy's big worry was his glove. If any one so much as touched it, much less pick it up, he went nuts, figured he'd make a bunch of errors that afternoon, sure as fate. An' most of the time, he did lose a throw or somethin' after his mitt had been monkied with—funny, huh?"

Then there were Hughie's thoughts on Amos Strunk, the center fielder and, in 1916, the best player on the worst team in Christendom.

Strunk was even worse. He'd buy a pack of chewin' gum and give it to me, tellin' me to give him one piece every day till it ran out. He always made me keep the glasses that he kept the sun off with too, and if any other guy took 'em up he was done with 'em; the glasses, I mean, and sometimes the fellow himself.

Nothing and no one amused Hughie more than Hughie did.

"He gave one of his famous chuckles, which is peculiar in that it more resembles a series of squeaks than a sound of mirth," wrote McCurley.

"He radiates sunshine incessantly."

And why not? He was the lucky mascot for a team that had no luck at all, at least as far as the standings were concerned, and no one seemed to mind.

* * *

That same season, a cloud threatened McLoon's radiance. "Virtually the entire Pennsylvania border is now being patrolled on the north, east, and south . . . a rigid quarantine at all railroad and ferry stations and highway approaches to the city . . . Schoolboys turned back to New Jersey . . . city authorities continuing efforts to stamp out the scourge . . . everywhere a horror."

The scourge was infantile paralysis, untreatable, misunderstood, terrifying. Decades earlier, constant exposure to the street filth that had earlier disgusted Dr. Arthur Ames Bliss in the Philadelphia slums years may in fact have protected the city's children from polio. But in the hottest month of 1916, in a wealthier, more sanitary city of cleaner streets, laundered sheets, and indoor plumbing, the virus took revenge. By mid-August, twenty-five infants and toddlers were dead, and new cases were being reported at a rate of one per hour.

"Moving-picture theater managers are co-operating by barring children under the age of 16," said the newspapers.

"Sand-piles in playgrounds are being disinfected, as are all breeding grounds for flies. . ."

"The ravages of the plague are not confined to this city . . . railroads to cooperate by the frequent fumigation of cars, with a special view to killing flies, either by disinfection or by 'swatting.'"

Leading Philadelphia's crusade against poliomyelitis was Dr. Wilmer Krusen, Director of Health and Charities, the same humanitarian who ordained that "persons who are knowingly affected with disease . . . owe it to themselves and to the human race to forgo the right of parentage" for the higher purpose of "preventing the production of crippled and physically hampered offspring."

In late August there was worse news. A forty-one-year-old woman, the first known adult patient, was "puzzling physicians of the city." Her case presented "another phase of the quarantine." Police were assigned to watch all quarantined homes.

At this terrifying hour, Elizabeth Geatens, age thirty-four, had a nine-year-old daughter named Dorothy in the house on Daly Street. Connie Mack had three young daughters at home, another child on the way, a one-year-old grandson, and a new mascot who revered him as much as his children did. By late fall, all of these would be spared. All would walk upright through the remainder of their lives, except for Hughie, whose fate it was to be crippled in advance.

* * *

Woodrow Wilson, campaigning on the manifesto of "America First" and slinging the trenchant slogan "He kept us out of war," won re-election in 1916 by one of the narrowest margins in American history.[20]

In late winter, as the scourge of polio finally retreated, Wilson's militant pacifism was tenuous and the A's, either with or without

---

20 The story is told that, when Charles Evans Hughes, "the bearded iceberg," Supreme Court justice, "animated feather duster," and former governor of New York, went to bed on the night of November 7, 1916, he believed that he had won the White House. "The President is asleep," Hughes's secretary supposedly told a reporter the next morning. "When he wakes up," said the scribe, "tell him he's not the President.")

mascot McLoon (there is no evidence either way), journeyed to Jacksonville for spring training with nowhere to go but up.

"Should all Connie Mack's youngsters be called away for military training," needled Ring Lardner, "the team would be vastly improved."

As training camp broke, so did President Wilson's patience. On April 2, 1917, he called a joint session of Congress and requested a formal declaration of war against the Kaiser: "The world must be made safe for democracy. Its peace must be planted upon the tested foundations of political liberty. We have no selfish ends to serve. We desire no conquest, no dominion."

In Philadelphia, thousands of citizens swarmed Independence Square under the banner of the Home Defense Committee. At the same time, ten thousand children were mustered into Washington Square to stomp with forty-eight-star flags beneath the leafless trees. "Around the city at locations where the President's Proclamation was read aloud there was little cheering or outbursts of patriotic enthusiasm," the newspapers reported.

"Philadelphians, Christian and Jew, appeared somber but with a silent determination to bear the coming trial with the help of God. It must not be forgotten that today is Good Friday. For Jews it is also the first day of Passover."

At a post office on Market Street at Ninth, several men had lined up to enlist in the U.S. Army when "an unnamed German" passerby shouted, "To hell with the flag!"

"Lynch him!" the patriots clamored.

"As the German was being surrounded," the *Philadelphia Inquirer* said, "Police Reserve Officer Bartleson arrived. He broke through the crowd and grabbed the German. He took him to a nearby automobile which had an American flag in it. He commanded the man to 'kiss the flag.' At first the man hesitated but as the crowd started moving closer, he obeyed.

"At that a great cheer arose and Officer Bartleson told the German to 'beat it' and he scurried away."

At 10 o'clock on Monday morning, April 10, the day before the Athletics' home opener, eighteen tons of gunpowder detonated at Building F of the Eddystone Ammunition Plant near Chester, Pennsylvania. Like the bullied, striking seamstresses of 1910, it was a girl's army that manned the machines at Eddystone. Dozens were killed instantly. Forty thousand shells exploded at once in a no-man's-land of shrapnel through which firemen and police officers charged bravely to the rescue. Some of the victims were blown into the Delaware River. At least fifty were reduced to pulp and left in a common crater. When the final toll was counted, 139 were dead. Philadelphia blamed the Germans.

"All are agreed that the series of explosions was the work of an enemy of the American Government, and the American people," the *Inquirer* avowed.

"The very fact that the system of protection at Eddystone proved vulnerable to an outsider has brought to Philadelphia a keen, even startling realization of the rigid protective measures necessary if similar catastrophes are to be prevented."

Like polio the summer before, the invisible horror was everywhere. "Dangerous Germans" were arrested in Pittsburgh. At Susquehanna University, students who objected to a bonfire of the works of Goethe and Beethoven were doused with a fire hose "to cool their Teutonic ardor." In Bristol, Pennsylvania, twenty-five shipyard pile drivers of Finnish origin were fired because they were "rooting for the Kaiser."

Investigators soon learned that the actual trigger at Eddystone was an electrical short-circuit, not sabotage. The plant reopened two weeks later, but the city was unraveling. The descendants of the buried dead at Weccacoe were targeted next for destruction.

"Three more shot in Chester riots," screamed the Philadelphia *Press.* "Latest Victims All Colored—Mob Pursues One on Way

From Place of Employment and a Fusillade of Bullets Cuts Him Down . . . Threats Made By Whites That Disturbances Will Not Cease Until All of the Other Race Are Killed or Driven Out of Town".

The years of recrimination, retribution, and riot had begun. To be fifteen in Philadelphia in 1917 was to be a few years too old for pretend-parading in Washington Square and a few months too young to sign up for the slaughter Over There. It was to understand that the house that the grown-ups built for you was painted in colors of bigotry and conflict, that the rooms had no windows, and the closets were filled with monsters.

* * *

Play ball!

"Even in the face of tragedy, other areas of life go on," the city read in its papers the same day that the scorecard of the Eddystone dead was published. "The A's opened the season at Shibe Park against the Senators. Unfortunately they came up against Walter Johnson who, even though suffering with a bad cold, held the Mackmen to just 3 hits. Washington took the opener 3 to 0."

Ring Lardner had been prescient: the 1917 A's were no less dreadful than the year before. They won ten of their first thirty outings. They were tied for last by Memorial Day. The difference was that now no one joked that, unlike the Athletics, at least the *Deutschland* came up for air. Mack and Shibe had always eschewed advertising on the outfield walls, but now they relented, allowing the words "Enlist Now Your Country Needs You" to be painted on the unpadded concrete outfield wall.

"So you can see to what steps we have gone to stimulate enlistments," Mack preened.

As it had since the 1800s, blockaded from reality by the Ionic pilasters of Shibe Park's grand façade, baseball distracted and salved a stricken city. Despite the declaration of war, attendance at Athletics home games was up from the year before. "We wonder if you realize baseball thrives on war!" sang Ferdinand Cole Lane, PhD (Hon.), the editor of *Baseball Magazine.*

Baseball will do its bit at this critical time, not as a luxury but as a necessity. Baseball will furnish relief from the tense mental strain which awaits growing casualty lists. Baseball will give needed diversion to the soldier in the trenches, to the drafted man in the training camps, to the laborer and the artisan and the businessman in our cities.

Baseball, in short, will act as a national escape valve for feelings too strong to be suppressed. Baseball is as necessary in time of war as ammunition or khaki uniforms.

In 1917, it was not only a hunchbacked child who conveyed magic, it was the game itself. In a matter of months, Philadelphia had been paralyzed by polio, convulsed by ethnic violence, blanched by explosion, numbed by war. Yet that spring, the whole town was worried about this: Who swiped Stuffy McInnis's bat?

The trusty bat that had rested so comfortably on the first baseman's broad right shoulder had wandered from the clubhouse. It was a terrible blow.

"It took me all winter to design that bat," wailed Stuffy. "I had it evenly balanced and could hit any kind of pitching with it. It was the most perfect thing I had ever seen and I depended on it to bring me back to the .300 class in the league. That bat was too good to be true, and I suspect a spy swiped it to have it reproduced. I was forced to use another bat the past few days and my swatting average has suffered. My only wish now is that

I meet that guy some day when he is carrying my beautiful bat under his arm.

"That's my wish. All I want is to meet him. That's all."

McInnis did not find his bat but he soon had a dozen of his most perfect things woodworked to his specifications. He batted .303 for the year, a nifty average, without a single home run. The Athletics finished last for the third year in a row.

Hughie McLoon, meanwhile, had been hedging his bets. He would not get a share of any World Series revenue (ever) but back at school, in that other world where he lived in another house with another name, he again entered the *Inquirer* contest for a new gold watch. But close contact with the Pathetics had robbed their mascot of his magic. The final total at Our Lady of Mount Carmel for 1917: a lad named Paul Dowd, 2,760, Hugh Geatens, 23.

CHAPTER TEN

"Hughie Beware"

ONE APRIL MORNING, early in the 1918 baseball season, Hughie McLoon drew a bath. His Athletics, destined for their fourth consecutive eighth-place finish, were already an insurmountable five games behind the Red Sox with only 125 games to play. (The season had been clipped from 154 games to 130 as a hat-tip to the war.) The players were in Washington without their batboy and were being shut out, 1–0, leaving Shibe Park and its hot running water to the mascot alone. He had probably finished with his formal schooling. If you can't win a wristwatch, why bother?

Preparing his twisted frame for his ablutions, Hughie struck a match to ignite the pilot light of the clubhouse boiler. The boiler exploded sky-high, an Eddystone in miniature. The next day's headline: "Bat Boy Is Damaged."

"Hugh was taking a bath when the heater for the showers exploded," it was reported, "and pieces of flying wreckage and metal struck him and lacerated his flesh in several places, but not seriously.

"He had to be removed to a hospital and patched up. Hugh attended the Phillies-Boston game in the afternoon swathed in bandages."

The A's clubhouse was a mess but the talisman survived. When the Pathetics got back from their road trip to open their home schedule and Hughie rejoined his clients, it was like they never went away: they blew three out of four.

* * *

"Career of Any Mascot a Series of Worries," said the Philadelphia *Evening Public Ledger.*

> Take the case of Hughey McLoon, rated as the king of mascots. Hughey is a Quaker City product. He started his career with the Mt. Carmel A. A. He displayed such ability that he attracted the attention of Connie Mack and after much effort was persuaded to desert the amateurs and become an out-and-out professional. This was in 1914. Hughey joined the Athletics in 1915 and for three seasons suffered terribly. He was with the A's when they were losing and every mascot knows that there's nothing worse than trailing along with a trailer.

Except for the trailing along and the terrible suffering, nearly everything reported by the *Ledger* was incorrect. In a couple of years, the paper would take the only possible corrective action, importing Hughie McLoon to "run" its sports department.[21] Meanwhile, mascotry remained his vocation.

One of Hughie's closest attachments during his first two seasons with the Athletics was John Phelan "Stuffy" McInnis, the slick-fielding first baseman and last remnant of the dismembered $100,000

---

21 As one colleague said: "He was never happier than when he could slip into a newspaper office to pick out a few lines on a typewriter. And he wrote well, too, although the job of operating the machine was always a handicap and a struggle."

Infield. Stuffy, barely five foot nine and youthful in appearance, had once been mistaken for a mascot in a minor league game and ordered off the field. "Mascot nothing!" his manager exploded. "That's my shortstop!" But as the 1918 season unfolded, Stuffy was gone as well. After attempting unsuccessfully to get McInnis to accept a reduction of his $4,000 salary, Connie Mack traded him to the Boston Red Sox for an infielder named Gardner, and replaced McInnis with a first sacker from the Detroit Tigers named Burns. Mack was no fool. Burns, twenty-three, had a low number in the national draft lottery while McInnis was being measured for combat boots.

On April 24, a few days after Hughie's explosion, McInnis and the Red Sox visited Shibe Park for opening day. They threw their ace lefthander, a twenty-three-year-old named George Herman Ruth, at the woebegone Athletics. But a southpaw named Sylveanus Augustus Gregg, who was born in the state of Washington before Washington was a state, pitched a six-hitter for the A's. Ruth gave up a three-run homer to Stuffy's successor, George Henry Burns, Gregg struck out the Babe himself, and the Macks collected a game, 3–0.

"Little Hughie McLoon, the official mascot, had the hardest job of his young life on his hands," observed the Philadelphia *Public Ledger* when Gregg blanked the Red Sox, "for he didn't know what side to root for. Hughie met the new players for the first time yesterday and it was difficult for him to get acquainted.

"His friend and pal, Stuffy McInnis, was clad in a hostile uniform, as were Joe Bush, Wally Schang, and Amos Strunk. Hughie looked longingly at the Boston bench several times and found it hard to keep from going over there. He wanted to be with Stuffy and Joe but it was against the rules so he stuck."

* * *

By mid-1918, three hundred thousand American doughboys were disembarking every month for France. Through the previous season, professional baseball had tried to keep running around and around the bases with its head down, but Major General Enoch Herbert Crowder, Provost Marshal General of the Army, was now finally enforcing selective service and Secretary of War Newton Baker— "I'm so much of a pacifist, I'm willing to fight for it"—had issued his famous "Work or Fight" decree. Seventy-five percent of major leaguers were of draft age. The innocents' inning was over.

"After July 1," said Crowder's statement, "any registrant who is found by a local board to be a habitual idler or not engaged in some useful occupation shall be summoned before the board, given a chance to explain, and, in the absence of a satisfactory explanation, to be inducted into the military service of the United States.

"We shall give the idlers and men not effectively employed the choice between military service and effective employment. Every man in the draft age at least must work or fight."

To keep the theaters open, actors, musicians, and dancers were excluded from the draft. Millions of dollars in Liberty Bonds were sold at their performances. Domestic servants and hairdressers were not exempt. Caught in a rundown between exemption and induction were major-league baseball's four hundred. General Crowder intended that athletes be included in "Work or Fight" but Baker's War Department demurred: "No ruling as to whether baseball players or persons engaged in golf, tennis or any other sport come under the regulations regarding idlers and non-essential pursuits will be made until a specific case has been appealed to the provost marshal general's office."

The idea that baseball might be terminated for the duration of the war "came like a bolt of lightning from a clear sky to most of the baseball men," said the *New York Sun*. But with no closure ordered and the players in limbo, they began the season regardless. On the

Fourth of July, three American League teams stood within one game of each other. Hughie's Athletics, naturally, were not one of them.

Some players thought the war a higher calling than the ball field. From the Athletics of 1916, weak-hitting Otis Lawry, "the next Eddie Collins," and winless hurler Hesselbacher both donned the uniform, their diamond failings forgotten in the face of the German horde.

* * *

Meanwhile, dozens of other players were beginning to feel that their chances of visiting France as a guest of their Uncle Sam would be lessened if they left the clubhouse and took on what looked from a distance to be a war-related job. The shipyards in Boston and Philadelphia, frantically riveting a blue-water navy from scratch, offered the verisimilitude of patriotic duty, striking exactly the right balance of service and safety. Plus, if the player was lucky, he could keep right on playing ball on company time, staying in shape until the Kaiser threw in the towel.

Shoeless Joe Jackson was one of the first of the game's big stars to jump the gun, signing on as a painter at a Bethlehem Steel plant in Delaware. He played in the Bethlehem Steel Baseball League as a member of the Wilmington squad. Babe Ruth also grabbed a sinecure at Bethlehem, then conspicuously enlisted in the 104th Field Artillery Division of the New York Army National Guard "before a huge crowd in Times Square." But the Bambino would never set a spike in France.

More than twenty current or former Big Leaguers suited up in the eight-team Delaware River Shipbuilding League, one of several on the seaboard in the summer of 1918. Miller Huggins, manager of the New York Yankees, complained that the Bethlehem Steel Company was offering his players terms equivalent to what they earned in the majors. He said that one of his players "was offered more money for going to one of the Atlantic Coast shipbuilding yards to play baseball and learn a skilled trade than his American League baseball contract called for."

As the casualty lists from the furrows of France stunned the home front, and as anti-German hysteria and 17 percent inflation rocked Philadelphia, any man not advancing with the army's warriors in the Argonne Forest was suspected of slacking, the most damning insult of the age. Sport itself became suspect in a world gone insane.

"There is a growing feeling against all men who have sought and secured soft jobs of keeping out of the army or active duty with the navy," wrote the *Philadelphia Inquirer.* "Those ball players and athletes who have secured sinecures are no longer looked upon as heroes who gave up well-paying positions to serve their country. The demand is that these men are put to real work and no longer continue in positions which women are enlisting to fill. The clubs of the ship yard and steel leagues are gaining nothing in popularity by scouring the country for players and for managers for their teams."

Philadelphia sent sixty thousand men to the front, leaving behind an embittered, divided city. Mothers endured "Heatless Mondays" and "Wheatless Mondays and Wednesdays." A rumor spread that "enemy aliens were planning to buy up all condensed milk to starve American babies." Statues of Schiller, Goethe, and Bismarck were painted yellow. The school board banned the teaching of German. Even Santa Claus got the stink eye: "It is seldom that one hears, at this time, the name of Kris Kringle," noted the *Philadelphia Bulletin* at Christmas.[22]

Ballplayers who had joined the industrial leagues "should be yanked into the army by the coat collar," said Ban Johnson, the

---

22 One hundred and sixteen thousand American soldiers would die in the fighting; 1,399 of them were from Philadelphia, and most of those from the city's famous 79th Division.

founder and president of the American League and an Ohio lawyer who had declined to sign up for the Philippine Insurrection back in the day.

"It may surprise the professional ball players of the United States that the American soldiers now fighting in France do not hold them in high esteem," the *Public Ledger* reported in August. "They do not scramble for news of how the big-league races are going."

"The boys are generally incensed over the statements they read to the effect that ballplayers have sought work in munitions plants and shipyards, where they can keep on playing ball," the battle-wounded Lt. Harry "Moose" McCormick, formerly a Giants' outfielder, said on a visit to New York after being injured at the front. "The feeling is so intense over there that *The Stars and Stripes*, the soldiers' paper, has stopped printing the big league scores and standings. The soldiers feel there has been too much evasion . . . by the ball players when other men, just as good, have gone into the big game."

* * *

Ring Lardner's character Jack Keefe also enlisted in the army in the final set of *You Know Me Al* stories, even though his manager warned him that "you won't last long over there because the first time they give you a hand grenade to throw you will take your windup and lose a hand."

A few nights later, Jack and Florrie put their little son Al to bed and tell him that his Daddy, like so many Daddies of so many little boys and girls, is leaving in the morning for the war.

"He says 'Can I go to Daddy?' How's that for a 3 year old Al?"

Not all of baseball's warriors were fictional. Late in the 1918 season, Mathewson and Cobb, along with Branch Rickey and George Sisler from the misbegotten Browns, reported for duty and were inveigled into the army's Chemical Warfare Service, formally the

30th Engineer Regiment (Gas and Flame). The unit's commander reasoned that "we do not just want good young athletes . . . we are searching for good strong men, endowed with extraordinary capabilities to lead men during gas attacks."

"We wound up drilling the darnedest bunch of culls the world war one army ever grouped into one outfit," Cobb wrote much later in *My Life in Baseball.* "The theory was that they would listen to well-known sport personalities, and to some extent it was effective. Those that gave us trouble and didn't heed orders didn't last long, for we weren't fooling around with simulated death when we entered those gas chambers."[23]

Major Mathewson and Major Cobb sailed to France in September. There, a gas-mask training exercise with real poison went wrong.

"Men screamed to be let out when they got a whiff of the sweet death in the air," Cobb wrote. "They went crazy with fear and in the fight to get out jammed up in a hopeless tangle . . . I fixed my mask, groped my way to the wall and worked through the thrashing bodies to the door. Trying to lead the men out was hopeless. It was each one of us in there for himself."

Cobb staggered to safety, but the great Giants pitcher would not make it. "I recall Mathewson telling me 'Ty, I got a good dose of the stuff, I feel terrible.' He was wheezing and blowing out congested matter. I saw Christy Mathewson doomed to die."

* * *

Staffed with misfits not wanted in France, major-league baseball carried on in 1918 as a cheer and distraction against the war's awful knell. Attendance at Shibe Park sometimes exceeded ten thousand. The city, and the country, had much to forget for an afternoon.

23 Cobb, Ty, *My Life In Baseball* (Lincoln, University of Nebraska Press, 1993).

The Mackmen's new star was pitcher Scott "Rope" Perry, a Texas ditch-digger, truck driver, and boozer who bounced around the industrial leagues of the heartland with a wife named Beulah and a battery of children, joining teams, abandoning teams, grabbing a buck and a bottle wherever he would. To an adoring Hughie McLoon, he must have seemed a creature from another world.

The Athletics were Perry's fourth big-league club in four years. He started thirty-six games in 1918 and completed thirty of them, pitching more innings than any other hurler in the American League and recording twenty-one of the A's fifty-two victories. After four years in the hardball wilderness, with the country and city at war, he gave the Lehigh Avenue rooters something to believe. "Every time he walks to the tee it is the signal for a wild demonstration," enthused *The Sporting News*.

Then Major General Crowder tightened the screws of "Work or Fight." Reluctantly, the major leagues prepared to go dark beginning July 21, Hughie McLoon's sixteenth birthday. Mack scheduled a farewell doubleheader against Cleveland for July 20. After winning the first game, the Athletics fell behind, 9–1, in the nightcap. Disgruntled fans poured from the terraces and hurled seat cushions at each other along the first and third-base lines.

In the weeks before this hiatus, the A's had enjoyed, or endured, a twenty-three-game home stand against six of the AL's other seven teams. (Travel was being restricted to save coal.) The umpires for the entire stretch were the same Silk O'Loughlin who had arbitrated the A's victory over Cleveland on the day that Hughie McLoon was born, and George Moriarty, former third baseman for the Detroit Tigers and Chicago White Sox.

According to one old yarn, Moriarty once called a strike on a pitch that Babe Ruth thought was wide:

"How do you spell your name?" asked Ruth.

"M-O-R-I-A-R-T-Y," answered the ump.

"Just as I thought. Only one 'I.'"

Moriarty was a grade-school dropout, a referee, a fist-fighter, a news-paper columnist and a rather successful pop-music lyricist, crafting eulogies for fallen athletes and stanzas for such tunes as Richard Whiting's touching "Love Me Like the Ivy Loves the Old Oak Tree":

> Love me like the ivy loves the old oak tree
> Make a vow and tell me how you'll always cling to me.
> Promise we will never sever—say you'll cling to me forever
> And love me like the ivy loves the old oak tree.

Something occurred during Moriarty's long summer sojourn at Shibe Park to awaken his ire. One August evening, following a dou-bleheader against St. Louis, the *Public Ledger* printed a vindictive poetic slander of the Athletics' batboy, written by Moriarty himself, complete with a photo of the grinning imp in oversized catcher's gear. The stanzas cast Hughie not as a luminous waif but in a darker light, as a pitiless dugout baiter and heckler. They also hinted that Moriarty had gained secret knowledge of Hughie's romantic attach-ments from third baseman Larry Gardner and catcher Cy Perkins.

> To the Athletics' Little Mascot,
> By an American League Umpire
> HEY HUGHEY McLOON!
> By George J. Moriarty
>
> Hey, Hughey McLoon, now you'd better watch out,
> I'm three times as mad as a guy with the gout;
> It didn't take Silk and me long to get wise

That you were no friend of us umpiring guys.
The first thing you know, one of these summer days,
There'll be a new mascot at work for the A's.

Hey, Hughey McLoon, all that rough stuff must go;
I guess you think I am a vaudeville show.
I saw you last week, you were howling with glee
Because that foul tip nearly busted my knee.
If I catch you laughing at me any more
I'll have to get waivers on you by the score.

Hey Hughey McLoon, I know all your dislikes;
You don't like to hear the A's called out on strikes
For when they go back you say, "Oh, never mind,
'Wot kin you expect from an umpire wot's blind?"
Hey, Hughey McLoon, guess you think yourself smart,
A 'buttin' in, taking the ballplayers' part.

Hey, Hughey McLoon, I could make you feel blue
If I cared to gossip or tattle on you;
What Gardner and Perkins told me all about
Would ruin a mascot if it should leak out;
But when there's a girl's name mixed in the affair
It's none of my business; but, Hughey, beware!

Nothing else would ever be printed about this poetic kneecapping, or the hinted romance. But it is clear that George Moriarty did not love the batboy like the ivy loves the old oak tree, and for McLoon, this would be the beginning of the end. Within two weeks, Hughie had left Connie Mack's Athletics. On August 9, the *Chester Times* had him mascotting and managing a team of "rivet heaters" in the Delaware River Shipbuilding League. He may have been doing his part in the plant and drawing a real paycheck. In any event, he would never tend the willows at Shibe Park again. The A's were perfectly able to finish last without him.[24]

* * *

On November 11, 1918, the Western Front fell quiet, at least for twenty-one years. The surviving doughboys brought home with them the wounds both physical and internal that would kill them young, or haunt their every elder day, the cynicism that would make a joke of Prohibition, and, in their lungs, the Spanish Flu.

Like poliomyelitis two years earlier, the "influ" brought Philadelphia to its knees in grief and terror, killing two, then five, then six, then seven hundred citizens a day through the ghastly autumn. The healthiest died first. The killing was so quick that bodies overflowed the morgue. A city lot at Second and Luzerne was turned into a mass grave. It was the Great War's final and most terrible barrage.

"People are stricken on the streets or while at work," reported the Surgeon General of the United States, Rupert Blue. "First there is a chill, then fever with temperatures from 101 to 103, headache, backache, reddening and running of the eyes, pains and aches all over the body, and general prostration. Persons so attacked should go to their homes at once, get into bed without delay and immediately call a physician."

"200,000 Cases in City," read a headline that quoted Dr. Wilmer Krusen, the indestructible director of health. Even the act of calling

---

24 As soon as the Athletics' season ended, Scott Perry followed Hughie to the docks. No mention of the mascot's departure from Major League Baseball ever reached the papers, which were focused on the fighting Over There, and race riots Over Here. Perry would be back pitching with the Mackmen the next April. He would lose forty-two more games the next two years.

a physician became nearly impossible. Eight hundred operators—27 percent of the work force—were out sick, or dead. Schools shut their doors. Churches were closed on Sundays for the first time in a generation. The entire liquor trade was shut down, including breweries, distilleries, retail establishments, restaurants and bars; a foretaste of Prohibition even as Congress debated the law.

Among the dead at Camp Dix, New Jersey, was Hugh Brown, Hughie's first cousin. Among the dead were the umpire Silk O'Loughlin and Connie Mack's brother Tom. Among the spared was a crippled boy growing to manhood at a terrible time. As the Great War ended and the influenza finally subsided, Hughie Geatens gave up his stepfather's name forever. In the 1920 census and on the streets of his native city he was a McLoon again, officially and forever.

Hughie McLoon (right) shakes hands with Connie Mack, manager of the Philadelphia Athletics

Peter and Elizabeth Geatens, Hughie McLoon's stepfather and mother

[Above] Connie Mack (centre), mastermind behind the Athletics and their great success — as well as the inventor of some of baseball's many dirty tricks

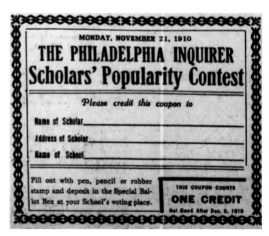

Coupon for the student popularity contest that Hughie won with a staggering 30,090 votes

Louis Van Zelst, mascot for the Athletics from 1910 to 1914, when he was the most envied boy in the country

Shibe Park, opened in 1909, was the home of the Philadelphia Athletics from 1909 to 1954 and the Phillies from 1938 to 1970

Charles "Victory" Faust, the eccentric mascot convinced that it was his predestination to pitch the New York Giants to a world championship

Hughie (far left) with the Athletics in 1917, when they were last in the league

Eddie Bennett (right), mascot for the New York Yankees,
with Babe Ruth (centre) and other players

To the Athletics' Little Mascot, By an American League Umpire

HEY, HUGHEY McLOON!
By GEORGE J. MORIARTY

HUGHEY McLOON

Hey, Hughey McLoon, now you'd better watch out,
I'm three times as mad as a guy with the gout;
It didn't take Silk and me long to get wise
That you were no friend of us umpiring guys.
The first thing you know, one of these summer days,
There'll be a new mascot at work for the A's.

Hey, Hughey McLoon, all that rough stuff must go;
I guess you think I am a vaudeville show.
I saw you last week, you were howling with glee,
Because that foul tip nearly busted my knee.
If I catch you laughing at me any more
I'll have to get waivers on you by the score.

Hey, Hughey McLoon, I know all your dislikes;
You don't like to hear the A's called out on strikes,
For when they go back you say, "Well, never mind,
Wot kin you expect of an umpire wot's blind?"
Hey, Hughey McLoon, guess you think yourself smart,
A-buttin' in, taking the ballplayers' part.

Hey, Hughey McLoon, I could make you feel blue
If I cared to gossip or tattle on you;
What Gardner and Perkins told me all about
Would ruin a mascot if it should leak out;
But when there's a girl's name mixed in the affair
It's none of my business; but, Hughey, beware!

Umpire George Moriarty's vindictive poetic slander of Hughie, as it originally appeared in the Public Ledger, 1918

Max "Boo Boo" Hoff and his stable of boxers; the shy and impeccable Hoff was a gangster kingpin who practically controlled Philadelphia during the later years of Prohibition

Jack Dempsey (right) takes on Gene Tunney at Sesquicentennial Stadium in Philadelphia, 1926; the crowd of over 100,000 spectators boasted persons from every walk, avenue, and boulevard of life

Hughie with his boxer, "Lanky" Ralph
Smith, in 1927 — the papers had a field
day with the altitudinal differential
between manager and fighter

[Left] Edward P. Carney, the "Dancing Judge", wearing a trademark carnation in his lapel, 1928

[Right] This beer advertisement assures readers that if they only drink plain American beer, as baseball players do, they'll also be able to lead very temperate lives

An illustration from 1915 that showcases Billy Sunday's charismatic preaching style and fiery poses

Hughie's death certificate: he died August 9, 1928 at the age of 26, after he was found crumpled on the shoe-shop stairway outside his own tavern

Virginia Fineman, one of Hughie's employees, identified Hughie's assailants to police and gave up so much information that it was almost as if she had known what was coming before it happened

Suspects in Hughie's murder appear in Magistrate's Court, 1928; from left, Samuel "Shorty" Feldman, Francis Peterson, William Sachs, David Glass, and Jennie Brooks

Thousands of Philadelphians attended Hughie's wake and funeral procession, and he was remembered by floral tributes from Connie Mack and "Boo Boo" Hoff

CHAPTER ELEVEN

"Square On The Beezer"

T HE WAR WAS LONG OVER by 1921, and the Spanish Flu a ghastly memory. Prohibition was in effect nationwide and ignored in Philadelphia by the most bribe-happy police department in the hemisphere. With enough cash in his pocket to rent a room of his own, Hughie moved away from his mother and Peter Geatens to 1837 Mifflin Street. He had so thoroughly recovered from his childhood seesaw tumble that he was able to play a decent game of basketball in the Catholic church league, and a new world was opening.

McLoon had gained admittance to a more refined and genteel set than the cushion-heavers of Shibe Park, joining the repertory company of what the wise guys called *Caulifloria*: the bone-crushing craft of professional boxing. With the A's and Phillies both finishing last in each of the previous three seasons (making it seven in a row for the Pathetics), boxing had become the preferred sport of the City of Brotherly Love. At least when two local brawlers square off, one of them has to win.

First as a mascot, and soon as a legitimate professional manager and matchmaker, Hughie rose in the sport without ever stepping into the ring himself. He was nimble with a water bucket and handy with a towel in the corners of some of the greatest champions of the sport's golden age.

Hunchbacks were as much a part of boxing as they were of baseball. In Los Angeles in 1913, when a lightweight named José Ybarra, fighting under the racist *nom-de-boxe* of Mexican Joe Rivers, was said to have "pointed the prow" of his opponent Knockout Brown (real name: Valentine Braunheim), "into the linoleum" three times in the tenth round of a scheduled twenty-round fight, each man had a humpback in his corner. Brown entered the ring with "Tobey," whom he had imported all the way from New York. Mexican Joe was accompanied by Eddie Burnell, secured especially for the occasion to offset the supposed influence of Tobey. Backed by his rent-a-hump, Rivers triumphed despite an injured hand. Knockout was knocked out.

Free of his duties for the Athletics, Hughie was in demand by fighting men. For the nation's kyphotics, it was a seller's market. As early as 1920, Hughie was listed as mascot for the stable of boxers run by a Philadelphia promoter named Chick Jannetti. Among them was bantamweight Solly Epstein, who won a couple of "newspaper decisions" (when neither fighter's prow found the linoleum and sportswriters at ringside chose the winner) before managing no better than a draw with a fellow Hebrew named Johnny Samuels, who fought by the awful name of Battling Chink. Jannetti's brightest star, Tommy Loughran, the "Philly Phantom" was the future light-heavyweight champion of the world.[25]

Known to everyone in town from his years as batboy at Shibe Park, his gnomish reputation tainted neither by umpire Moriarty's unflattering poetry nor by the A's putrid performances, and with

---

25 In 2020, an historic sign outside the church remembered Loughran as "a gentleman both in and out of the ring." As for Jannetti, he would be shot to death while trying to break up a robbery at a blind pig in Wilkes-Barre, Pennsylvania, in 1931.

his grin as wide and winsome as ever, Hughie was keeping some very large company in the new decade. In 1921, the *Philadelphia Evening Public Ledger* had him negotiating with representatives of the "Manassa Mauler," heavyweight champion Jack Dempsey, to serve as mascot at his training camp in Atlantic City.[26] Dempsey was emerging, slowly, from the ignominy of being labeled the Great War's biggest slacker, a charge he disputed by producing a registration card from a draft board in San Francisco that showed the planet's most fearsome puncher categorized as an undraftable 4-F. (He claimed exemption as the sole support of his wife and mother.)

At the seashore, Dempsey was preparing to battle Georges Carpentier, France's gallant pilot of *la guerre de quatorze*. Their encounter in Jersey City, one of the first broadcast on radio, would be called the Fight of the Century (as would many to follow). The heavyweight champion passed over Hughie and chose instead to designate "King," his pit-bull terrier, as his official mascot: a decision the champ would regret a few months later, when King bit a child and brought Dempsey a $10,000 lawsuit.

As befit his status as Philadelphia's most famous hunchback, Hughie had been asked by two prominent Jewish boxers to serve as mascot for their upcoming world-title match. One was Lefty Lew Tendler, another fatherless South Philly boy, four years Hughie's senior. The other was Manhattan's Benny Leonard, an impoverished garment worker's son, the world lightweight champion, and an artful assassin who, a century later, remains ranked as one of the most dangerous professional punchers of any creed, weight, or epoch.

---

26 Hughie may or may not have sailed to Belgium with the U.S. Olympic boxers in 1920–probably not, since only one ambiguous newspaper clipping suggests it—which would have been just as well. One Philadelphia fighter who did make the voyage to Antwerp reported that "It wasn't exaggerated at all—that stuff about the food being 'fit for dogs.' It was terrible—and no worse than the decisions given by the judges during the boxing matches."

Leonard and McLoon already were in a relationship: Hughie was in Benny's corner when he out-pounded KO Willie Loughlin in Camden, New Jersey the previous November. A photograph taken about the time of the Loughlin fight shows Leonard, in a suit and bowler, embracing the beaming McLoon, who is wearing a double-breasted blazer and his trademark cloth cap. At five feet, five inches, the lightweight champion towers over his mascot by nearly a foot. Hughie McLoon looks happier than in any other recorded moment of his life. "I'm a championship mascot," Hughie declared, "and Leonard is my man."

At the same time that he was training to fight the unorthodox Lefty Lew, Leonard was battling it out with another formidable challenger—Bertrand Russell, philosophy's heavyweight titlist. Boxing, said Russell in an interview in the New York *World*, equals "sadism." Imprisoned for his pacifism during the Great War, Russell admitted that he never had been to a boxing match in his life. "It just never came my way," he shrugged. He denounced the sport for arousing "brutal emotions" and appealing to man's "lust for cruelty. The ordinary person has far more cruelty in his nature than he realizes. We go about looking for legitimate opportunities to satisfy it."

Benny Leonard counterpunched in the same newspaper, where he was a regular columnist:

Sadism does not exist in the ring more than it does in other rough sports, such as football, lacrosse, and hockey . . . the boxers have no malice in their hearts. They know that a blackened eye, a sore side, a broken nose, while it may hurt, seldom causes permanent injury. When they measure their opponent for the blow that deprives the rival temporarily of his senses, there is not the slightest bit of malice, and, in 99 of 100 cases, not the least bit of anger.

Russell jabbed back that fans complained of not getting their money's worth without a knockout: "The fighter with a paralyzing punch—a killer—is so much more popular than a clever boxer who lacks the knack of a knock out; it explains the crowd's savage roar of excitement when a hitter connects and his unfortunate victim staggers, groggy from the blow. The basic appeal of prize-fighting is to man's primitive sadism."

Leonard returned:

> Certainly it is not sadism when we shout with joy as the fullback of Notre Dame plows down the field, and several of the opposing line are stretched out on the field, their wits temporarily knocked out of them. That's not sadism; that's red-blooded American men and women venting their excitement in shouts at a great exhibition of sport.

Leonard was the leading contender to retain Hughie's mystic mascotry powers for his upcoming defense. But, at the same time, Hughie was seen in the papers posing with Lew Tendler and his entourage. The photo shows a dozen older, taller men in suits and straw boaters, and Hughie, in his cloth cap and that same pinstripe blazer, too short now for his gangling arms. The newspaper caption called him "McGloos." Lefty Lew was a natural-born Philadelphian, unlike the alien Gothamite Leonard. But no mascot could serve two masters.

In a syndicated newspaper article, the only McLoon byline extant, Hughie announced his decision: he would be in Benny Leonard's corner for the Tendler brawl. It is the best representation we have of Hughie's actual voice:

> Picking winners ain't just as soft as picking strawberries or nothing like that, but all the same I'm doping it out that Benny Leonard will sock Lew Tendler on the button hard enough and often enough to come through flying out at the Philly ball park

next Friday night. It's this way—Leonard's smarter than Tendler first of all. Leonard took me for mascot and that proves the kind of stuff under his noodle, while as to Tendler—the time he got up after Willie Jackson connected with his whiskers finished my idea that he was smart. Any guy that gets smacked like that and gets up, not knowing but what he's gonna get one harder yet, must be simple somewhere.

Also Tendler never boxed a bird that hit like Leonard, short and fast almost like one punch only there's anywhere from three to six. He's sure to get rattled and then Benny's prime to let him have it right square on the beezer. I remember reading at school how the English knew Washington was near them, but didn't know he was going to cross the Delaware. Well, it's just like that with these fellows. Tendler knows that right of Benny's is there, but he won't figure on the latter crossing it when he does. And he's going into another land when it does.

Not that Lew ain't a good fellow—he is; it's just that Leonard's got more class than he has. When Benny wings him it won't be no light tap that he can skin under or take smiling—it's gonna make him so light headed the rest will be easy. Benny ruins 'em, you know; he don't just beat 'em. And if he gets a chance to sock Tendler there ain't going to be no reason for a return match.

There'll be about sixteen gongs to the scrap, regular and nice, but after it there'll be about thirty more by the ambulance that's gonna be needed to get Lew somewhere that the treatment's good and quick. Benny's due for another home run and Tendler looks like a lively ball. That's the dope, about the sixth round.

Two days later, Benny Leonard wrote a public letter to McLoon:

My Dear Hughey: You are officially appointed my mascot for my coming fight with Lew Tendler. While I am not losing a great deal of sleep over the prospect of Tendler running away with my title, with you as my mascot, I won't lose.

It was all for naught. Just days before the title match with Tendler, Leonard dislocated his thumb in training by punching a sparring partner on the head. He suffered "intense pain" and was laid up in a plaster cast for six weeks. Privately, Bertrand Russell cheered.

"I am now under my mother's care," the lightweight champion assured a worried world. When he finally did meet Lefty Lew the following summer, Benny socked him square on the beezer often enough to win the decision.

* * *

Hughie was everywhere in the new decade, as an athlete, a promoter, a manager, a jinx-killer, a spectator, a hobnobber, a sportswriter, a "general handy man" of the Pennsylvania State Athletic Commission, a water boy, and as the protégé—later, the official salaried clerk—of a man named Edward P. Carney, who had been elected in 1919 to the position of magistrate at City Hall. Famous for the white carnation in his buttonhole and his indiscreet tongue, Carney, who once indicted and fined a tailor who overcharged him by a dime for pressing a suit, had known and loved Hughie since the hunchback was a child. It is likely that Hughie had been around City Hall with his father's cousin, Hugh Patrick McLoon, the taverner.

A brief catalogue of all the sporting enterprises that Hughie McLoon engaged in after leaving Connie Mack's Athletics must begin with the night in 1919 that he slicked one half of the basketball court at the Moose Hall on North Broad Street, just south of the Temple University campus (the teams were not yet in the habit of changing ends).

Hughie was mascotting the North Philadelphia team in the Eastern League of professional basketball in a match against St.

Philip de Neri. Basketball itself was less than thirty years old. To tilt the scales in his team's favor, just as Connie Mack used to tell his groundskeepers to let the grass grow tall at Shibe Park, Hughie greased the end of the playing surface where the de Neris would be shooting. Or, as the *Philadelphia Bulletin* reported: "Hughie McLoon, Connie Mack's pet mascot, tried his mystic charms with a bottle of olive oil."

It was a good night for North Philly. A center named Oscar Grimstad poured in a headline-grabbing seven buckets and the Norths coasted to victory, 42–29.[27] "Several sensational field goals," it was reported, "featured in the forty-minute tiff."

"De Neri's play was erratic at times," noticed the *Philadelphia Inquirer*. "There was a noticeable lack of cutting for the basket whenever a visiting player had the ball . . . The de Neris protested the game before it started. The floor was slippery. . ."

Two years later, Hughie was joyriding up Broad Street on a tractor as part of a carnival staged by the Downtown Jewish Orphans' Home. Some cretin hurled a rock at his head. "When the machine reached Broad and Porter Streets," reported the *Evening Public Ledger*, "a group of boys attempted to board it. Repulsed, they started throwing stones. McLoon fell off unconscious when a heavy piece of brick hit him on the head. He was taken to the Methodist Hospital and later sent home."

At the age of eighteen in November 1920, Hughie scored a team-high nine points at forward for the Mount Carmel Boys Club junior basketball team in a 28–15 loss to the Saranac Scouts. A week later, he played the full forty minutes and put up another nine-spot in a

---

27 Oscar "Swede" Grimstad, a combat veteran of the Great War, was "one of the most outstanding pivots" at the naissance of professional basketball, decades before the NBA. He died young, only forty-three, "of a complication of diseases," at home in the Mohawk Valley of New York State, "and he had not played his favorite game in a long time."

blowout by the Parkside Reserves. "McLoon excelled for the Mt. Carmel boys," noted the Camden *Courier.*

On the diamond, Hughie was "the shining star" of a youth team called the White Elephants, named after the fabled Mackmen to whom he brought no measurable luck at all. He made "several good catches." He hit the ball "with better than average ability." One of the other outfielders was named Geatens, perhaps a step-cousin, perhaps a coincidence.

If it did take Elizabeth Palmer McLoon Geatens seven years to teach her boy to walk again after his fall from the seesaw, she had done good work. Not yet twenty, he was a triple threat: basketball, baseball, business.

> Hughey McLoon's White Elephants, a traveling team, has been winning many games and has defeated some of the best teams in Philadelphia . . . The team would like to arrange games. Hughey McLoon, 1837 Mifflin St.

And:

> Hughey McLoon . . . has signed a number of star high and prep school players to represent him on the basketball floor, and is looking forward to a brilliant season . . . The team has several open dates for all first-class teams in and around the city willing to pay a reasonable guarantee. Hughey McLoon, 1837 Mifflin Street.

And:

> The Mount Carmel Boys Club . . . are out with challenges to all teams of that class. Manager Hughey McLoon, former mascot of the Athletics, wants to hear from all sixteen and

seventeen-year-old teams in the city, for games to be played either at home or away. For games address Hughey McLoon, 1837 Mifflin Street.

* * *

A headline in the *Philadelphia Inquirer* in August 1925 read: "Hughie McLoon Takes Title from Johnny Burns as Tiniest Manager."

"Without the aid of a left jab, or a double cross, Hughie McLoon yesterday won a title," the paper announced. A local promoter and booker of fistfights named Dougherty had gone off to the Golden State to arrange some bouts and left twenty-three-year-old Hughie in charge. The Johnny Burns referenced in the headline was a retired welterweight who had fought six times as a pro before switching to the cash end of the sport. "Hughie is now the smallest manager in the world," the paper said.

Managing a boxer in the 1920s meant issuing invitations to other fighters through the newspapers, always claiming that your man was the second coming of Jack Dempsey, yet allowing that he would stoop to pound any other agent's palooka if the price was right. Hughie sought to obtain a ten-round match for a lightweight named Alex Hart: "I am trying to get Jimmy Goodrich for Hart. But Goodrich either can't read, or else he is hard of hearing. He has not answered the challenge."

Hughie presented Hart as "a clever fistman" and next offered to take on a guy named Cooney, possibly across the Delaware. Cooney, came the response, was "ready to meet Hart or any other lightweight in the country, at any time and at any place." The bout was arranged, the contracts inked. Hughie jockeyed Alex Hart up to Newark to fight the amenable Cooney.

Alex Hart got knocked cold in the seventh round. He fought 153 times as a professional and died at the age of thirty-five, two years to the day after his last bout. Caulifloria is no country for old men.

* * *

One night in August of 1925 at the fights in Philadelphia, the A's announcer, Babe O'Rourke, whose own record as a professional boxer was zero victories and one loss by technical knockout, introduced Magistrate Edward P. Carney as "the real fighting champion." Carney and his trademark white boutonnière were running for re-election. "Judge Carney is in distinctly good with the sport lovers," wrote James Isaminger in the *Inquirer*.

Moments later, Hughie McLoon "scampered into the ring carrying a placard bigger than himself which read 'Stand by Magistrate Carney. Re-elect him.' Later on, the dashing young Carney, known as the 'Dancing Judge,' took a seat at the ringside and drew a big hand."

A few weeks later, Hughie showed up at City Hall to hand the Board of Elections no fewer than twenty-two thousand signed petitions, more than enough to ensure that Edward P. Carney's name would appear on the November ballot. That same morning, the *Inquirer's* headline above the day's political news was "Warrants Issued For Ballot Crooks." The article stated that attorney Algernon R. Clapp, representing a defeated but cheated Independent candidate, was in possession of "irrefutable evidence of fraud in the West Philadelphia bailiwicks. They declare they will be able to prove that in these, and in other divisions of the city, the vote returned exceeded the registration." At some locations, as many as 210 more votes were reported than there were living voters on the rolls.

"Independents," the newspaper said, "were sure that the District Attorney would quickly seize upon any opportunity to get in on the ground floor and deliver a knockout blow to the plunderers of the ballot box." But the District Attorney never did. Only the Independents cared.

Philadelphia was booming. Connie Mack's A's were back on the ascendant, finishing in second place with 88 victories, their best record since the death of Louis Van Zelst. Conductor Leopold Stokowski was in residence at the Academy of Music, the great Museum of Art was under construction on the Parkway, and the American Sesquicentennial was only months away. The jazz was hot, the town wide open, and the armies of law enforcement and illicit pleasure raised a toast to each other's health.

"Philadelphia," bragged the *Bulletin Year Book* for 1926, "with approximately one-sixtieth of the nation's population, produces one-quarter of all American-made goods." The paper had the statistics to back it up: 45,000,000 yards of carpet; 3,079,476,220 cigarettes; 53,770,000 ice cream cones; 83,862,700 false teeth.

In the middle of it all, equally at home in the stadiums and the speakeasies and City Hall, was Hughie McLoon. He was "the wing-footed Mercury who carries the news of boxing events to come to the various public prints." He was "known to perhaps as many sport followers, partisans, and performers as any young man now on Mother Earth." He was the victor in the Philadelphia Sporting Writers Pocket Billiard Tournament at the National Academy. In his double-breasted pinstripe jacket, size XXS, he squired Jack Dempsey around a professional wrestling match. "McLoon," said Magistrate Carney, "is my lucky stone."

CHAPTER TWELVE

"She Was Cremated"

IT WAS A BOOZY WINTER Saturday night, six years into Prohibition and halfway through what would be the short life of the reverent, ridiculous crusade, when a bunch of frightened flappers, drunk as skunks, raced across a roof at Spruce and Twenty-Fourth. The Quaker City was ground zero for the resistance.

Five carloads of policemen closed in on a residence they described as a "'Kaffie Klatch'—a 'wild party' house for paid guests":

> Girls obviously under the influence of liquor reeled about in the embrace of their escorts to the tune of wild jazz symphonies . . . The interior of the building was outfitted sumptuously. The front room was reserved for dancing. At the rear, heavy carpets padded the floor and divans almost buried beneath gaudy and fancy cushions on the 'sidelines' gave an Oriental effect.

The "motor patrols" pulled up in front, continued the *Philadelphia Inquirer*:

> Silently they surrounded the house and at a signal made a concerted rush on the building . . . Fifteen girls and youths fled to

the roof through a trap door, and led the raiders a chase around chimneys and even neighboring roofs before they were finally captured.

Girls who had brazenly snapped their fingers in the faces of the police sobbed hysterically as they were led into the patrols, followed by their awed and frightened escorts. In the excitement that followed the rush of police and detectives into the establishment the alleged proprietor disappeared.

Hurried telephone calls brought Hugh McLoon, clerk in the office of Magistrate Carney, to the station house a half-hour later. He secured copies of the charges for all the prisoners and shortly after returned with the orders for the release of the captives.

Welcome to the Roaring Twenties.

* * *

"The reign of tears is over," Billy Sunday had exulted in Norfolk, Virginia, as the Eighteenth Amendment took effect in January 1920. "The slums will soon be only a memory. We will turn our prisons into factories and our jails into storehouses and corn-cribs. Men will walk upright now, women will smile, and the children will laugh. Hell will be forever for rent."

"Drink, consoling friend of a Perturbed World, is shut off," lamented Franklin Lane, who had been Wilson's Secretary of the Interior, in contrariety, now that his own interior was legally limited to buttermilk. "And all goes merry as a dance in hell!"

Both were wrong. "N.Y. is some dry town . . . and the only way a man can get a drink here is to go to a saloon," wrote Ring Lardner's Jack Keefe to his friend Al, "and the only differences between old times is what they soak you for it now which is plenty but when a man had got to have it he has got to have like today after the game for inst. my old stomach was fretting mighty bad and I got myself 6 high balls on the way back from the pk. and it set me back $2.40 but as I say what is $2.40 compared to a man's health."

Bad as New York was, Philadelphia was worse: the laughingstock of the nation. "Philadelphia," said one official trying to dry out the city, "is in the position of a very rich man who wants a physician to fix up his liver trouble so he can go at it again."

"There is no doubt," reported the New York *Herald Tribune,* "that Philadelphia is now experiencing the travails of another Chicago. The beer and alcoholic gangs have been having lively times in the town within the last two years, sending twenty-five of their number to violent deaths. . . . Like their fellow keg toters of the Windy City, they have a predilection for handling high-powered beer and have organized its distribution to an amazing degree . . . Their profits, it is said, run monthly into the hundreds of thousands of dollars."

Emulating King Canute, the paper continued, Philadelphia's Mayor Mackey "stretched forth his hand in heroic gesture and ordered the tide to stop . . . As in the case of his ancient predecessor, the flood continued on its course."

* * *

The instrument by which Philadelphia's mayor intended to stop the tide was U.S. Marine Corps Brigadier General Smedley Darlington Butler, a.k.a. the Fighting Quaker, a.k.a. Old Gimlet Eye. The descendant of a Society of Friends patriarchy from West Chester, Pennsylvania, that was so hidebound and venerable that Butler's father addressed him as "thee," General Butler was one of the most decorated combatants and leaders of men in the proud annals of the Leathernecks, a two-time winner of the Medal of Honor for actions in Mexico and Hispaniola.

The first medal was won in 1914 at Veracruz, during the U.S. invasion during the civil wars that followed the Mexican Revolution, when "Butler went ashore in command of a company of sailors and a company of Marines from another battalion. As his force moved into the city, hidden riflemen pinned them down. Armed with only a swagger stick, Butler calmly walked down the center of the main street fully exposed."

Informed that he had been given the U.S. military's ultimate commendation for bravery under enemy fire, the Fighting Quaker "refused the award and sent it back. The Navy Department returned the medal to Butler, testily ordering him to accept and wear it."

The second medal was conferred after he led a squad of 96 Marines against a force of several hundred Haitian insurgents holed up in an old French fortress during a rebellion in 1915. Sneaking into the bastion through a sewage pipe, Butler's men annihilated fifty of the enemy and seized the stronghold. The only cost to the American contingent came when some renegade threw a rock and knocked out a Marine's front teeth.

In 1923, the redoubtable Butler was on his way home from a college football game in New York to his headquarters at Quantico, Virginia, when he was asked to pause in Philadelphia for a talk with Mayor W. Freeland Kendrick.

"He looked over the available stock of generals," Butler told Lowell Thomas in *Old Gimlet Eye: The Adventures of Smedley D. Butler*. "I was the only one eligible. The meeting was arranged with considerable secrecy in a room at the Bellevue-Stratford Hotel. Kendrick enlarged on the crime conditions in Philadelphia, on the banditry that held sway and the poison liquor that was killing scores, and wound up by offering me the post of Director of Public Safety."[28]

---

28 Thomas, Lowell, *Old Gimlet Eye: The Adventures of Smedley D. Butler* (Burtyrki, 2020).

Defiant and fearless in combat even though he was shorter than Benny Leonard, General Butler had not read his Steffens: "I was innocent enough to believe that the administration intended to carry out its pledges to clean up the city," he would confess much later. "To wage ruthless war on crime and vice and to enforce prohibition. Before I was handed my hat and shown the door, I knew better. I was hired as a smoke screen. I was to make a loud noise, put on a brass hat, stage parades, chase the bandits off the streets—and let vice and rum run their hidden course. The whole history of my two years in Philadelphia is filled with incidents of people approving my work until it interfered with their own violation of the law."

The first thing Butler did on assuming his directorship was to haberdash a suitable costume for himself—nothing too gaudy or showy, just a muted reflection of his integrity and intentions. "He took the oath in his Marine uniform," said the *Philadelphia Record*, "but reappeared a half-hour later in a uniform he himself had designed, blue with gold trim, its cape, taken from his Marine mess jacket, revealing a flaring red lining. He called the police inspectors to his office and told them that the lieutenants in forty-two districts were to 'clean up in forty-eight hours or face immediate demotion.'"

The second thing the leatherneck did was hire ex-batboy Hughie McLoon to be his personal process server, secret agent, and "smeller," a private nose able to discern with one quick snort whether the colorless liquid in a society woman's fish tank was water or a Tom Collins.

Magistrate Carney, whom Hughie still served as sidekick and surrogate son, was also in the enforcement racket, with a varying degree of whole-heartedness, making the Fighting Quaker and the Dancing Judge nominal allies in the prosecution of Pennsylvanians who resorted to a consoling friend in a moment of perturbation. They had little else in common, other than inestimable self-confidence and showy wardrobes.

The Dancing Judge, in the "gorgeous champagne-colored shirts that have elevated him in the eyes of the city's Beau Brummels," greeted everyone he met with a smile, a hearty handclasp, and the words "I'm your friend, Eddie Carney." By contrast, Butler had greeted every stranger he encountered in his old job with a bayonet. To keep his magistracy, Carney needed to maintain the confidence of the common citizen; thus, the presence of Hughie McLoon in the boxing ring with the "Re-Elect Carney" sign. Butler answered only to Mayor Kendrick, who, when perturbed, was known to say, "I was brave enough to hire General Butler, and I'm brave enough to fire him." Despite Carney and Butler's theoretically shared goal of rigidly enforcing the laws of city, commonwealth, and country, there would be friction between them.

In the first flush of his authority, Butler, who had a gigantic representation of the Marine Corps' Eagle, Globe and Anchor emblem tattooed across his upper body (although a swath of South America had been gouged out by a deflected bullet in Tianjin during the Boxer Rebellion in 1900), commanded his bluecoats to raid as many of the city's speakeasies as they could in a two-day period. Nine hundred and seventy-three establishments were forced to close their doors.

For a few hours. The Venice Café, raided five times in those two days, and hit twice more later in the week, remained open. "Sure, we got beer," a bartender told the press.

A few days into the brigadier's blitz, Butler and Carney got into a tiff. When a constable requested a warrant to enter and search a home from which he had seen people teeter in a state of obvious drunkenness, Carney turned him down. The mayor convened a meeting at which Carney declared, "Let's get this straight first. Do you advise us if people come out of a house drunk, to issue a warrant? They may be guests or relatives, how do we know? If that's so, we're all breaking the law from the Mayor on down. I know I've got liquor in my house and heaven help the cop who tries to get it!"

No one ever accused Edward Carney of being averse to a convivial nip. One night in the winter of 1925, the Dancing Judge and Hughie were both in attendance at a lavish dinner at the Piccadilly Café at Broad and Spruce, an establishment where, according to the *Inquirer*, "the bootlegging elite gathered of nights and made the welkin ring with their revelry." The soirée had been called in celebration of the acquittal in court of a group of boatmen accused of towing a barge laden with $300,000 worth of imported liquors to a berth on Rancocas Creek, over on the Jersey side. Honored guests included former Congressman Benjamin M. Golder, Republican of the Fourth District, a regular consort and retainer of the rum-running aristocracy:

> Wine flowed in sufficiency to put an ancient Roman orgy to the blush. A veteran waiter, who told about it all, said that in his twenty-three years of serving where liquor was dispensed he never saw so much wine before.

Twenty-five cases of champagne were brought in to wash down the victuals. One employee later testified that the café's owner, afraid that the servers themselves would get too wasted to wait, promised each man two quarts of liquor if they remained sober.

"And did he keep his promise?"

"He did. We each got two quarts—and drank them, too."

"Sherman was right about war," sighed Butler, "but he was never head of the police in Philadelphia."

* * *

Magistrate Carney had no intention of wringing every last drop of alcohol out of Philadelphia. Drinking it, maybe; wringing it, no. But if he and Butler agreed on anything, it was that the smallholders of the city's estimated thirteen thousand speakeasies, party houses, and holes-in-the-wall should not bear the burden of prosecution while the big hotels and the Piccadillies served their scotch scot-free. It offended their sense of justice. And it made political sense: as they said in Philly, one man, three or four votes.

It was in this spirit that Carney and Butler agreed to raid the Ritz-Carlton and, if alcoholic beverages were discovered on the premises, withdraw the hotel's dancing license and padlock the old dump. By "the premises," Butler said, "I mean the whole hotel. Something must be done to teach these big fellows that they must obey the law as well as the little fellows."

"Feeding young girls wine and punch in fashionable hotels has got to stop," Butler seethed.

"'Jazzing them up a bit,' they call it. I call it a disgrace, and I believe the American people would see the Ritz-Carlton torn down stone by stone rather than allow such conditions to go on. I am going to make an issue of it and see if the people of Philadelphia will stand back of me."

The raid went down on Wednesday evening, December 5, 1925. Carney handpicked a brigade of his "youngest and handsomest officers" to encircle a private party in the ballroom and dining rooms on the second floor of the grand hostelry.

Two other young men were deputized to disguise themselves as waiters: a part-time stage actor named John T. Muldoon, described as "23-years-old, slight of stature," and Hughie McLoon, of the same age. Muldoon went in first. McLoon backed off—some of the guests recognized him as the process server from a similar raid on the Club Madrid a few weeks earlier.

Everything came out four days later at the police station at Twelfth and Buttonwood, in a hearing "replete with farcical scenes and burlesque wordy battles" at which Edward P. Carney, "the stormy petrel of Philadelphia's minor judiciary," served as witness, prosecutor, and judge in his own raid. It was during these proceedings that Carney released the manager of the Ritz-Carlton on bail, pointed his "pudgy index finger" at witnesses, charged that the police were "making suckers out of the poor people" by hauling them in for minor liquor offenses while ignoring booze-soaked bacchanals at the poshest hotels, "and then, as his real climactic feature, issued a vehement challenge to General Butler, who was not there, to debate with him on the merits and demerits of the prohibition laws."

"Hugh McLoon, official smeller in the Ritz raid," was called as a witness, wrote the *Inquirer*, noting that Hughie was no longer the mascot of the Athletics. "About ten years ago he had served in that capacity for a short time," Connie Mack told the paper, keeping his distance from the boy he once embraced.

A solicitor named Abbott defended the Ritz and a lawyer named Gray attacked McLoon, who was described by the paper as "a hunchback and under medium height."

When McLoon said he was a clerk in Carney's office, Gray asked sarcastically if the magistrate ever entered it himself.

"Once in a while," answered McLoon, airily.

Hughie told the court he had been waiting with Magistrate Carney at the Sylvania Hotel while Muldoon "looked for evidence" at the Ritz-Carlton. He then ventured over to the Ritz at about 12:50 a.m., and saw men and women staggering off the elevators.

"These people seemed intoxicated, for I'm sure the dancing didn't do it," said McLoon.

"You can't tell these days, what with the Charleston and that new tango," interposed Abbott.

"When I got in the place, I heard a woman say 'Carney's here,' and there was a lot of excitement," McLoon continued. "A man was instructing his guests to go out the Broad Street door, as the Walnut Street exit had been closed. Every elevator brought more staggering men and women in evening clothes down to the ground floor. They stumbled down into the lobby."

"Are you sure they were intoxicated?" asked Abbott.

"Sure," said McLoon. "They nearly knocked me down."

"With their bodies or with their breaths?"

"With their bodies, of course, for they were physically drunk. I found twelve full bottles of champagne in Room 201, in a grip, and four bottles of Scotch liquor under a table. In the pantry I saw ice in a sink and two empty champagne bottles on a table. On tables and on the floor of Room 201, I saw about fifty empty bottles, and empty bottles and glasses piled on a women's dressing table. I saw a woman's grey fur coat tossed over a table.

"In the center of the room I saw two tables that had been made into a bar."

"How many bottles did you see altogether?" Abbott asked.

"About fifty or sixty. I only counted the full bottles. When the police came, Magistrate Carney told me to give the suitcase with the twelve bottles of champagne to a policeman, and instructed me to follow him. Mr. Carney said, 'You remember what happened last time, so keep your eye on it.' I followed the cop right down to the wagon on Broad Street and told him to put it on the sidewise seat and sit alongside it.

"While I was watching the suitcase a man in the crowd said 'I'd give $500 to get the suitcase' and someone said to him 'Why don't you steal it yourself?' I told him to move on or I'd have him locked up.

"Did you see any drunken women on the second floor?" Carney asked.

"Yes," said McLoon. "I saw one who was drunk."

"How far gone was she?"

"Oh—she was cremated," said Hughie, producing a roar of laughter in court.

"He means ossified," prompted Mr. Abbott.

"Do you know who this woman was?" asked Carney.

"No," said McLoon, "she had on a fur coat and I couldn't tell if she were a guest or a maid. Everybody wears a fur coat nowadays."

* * *

Within a week, Brigadier General Butler's furniture was stacked on the porch of the house he was renting at 2325 North Fifty-Eighth Street in Overbrook, "under the direction of Mrs. Butler."

"I have learned a lot in my two years in public office," he said in parting. "I have learned to believe nothing that anybody says about me and to say nothing that I mean . . . You have taken me and kicked me and dragged me to death."

"Cleaning up Philadelphia," he added, "was worse than any battle I was ever in."

Returning with relief to the United States Marine Corps, Butler chose an easier assignment: the Chinese Civil War.

"He was honest," eulogized the *Philadelphia Record*. "That was taken for granted or he wouldn't have been appointed. But he was 100 per cent honest. We think we are doing the Mayor no injustice in expressing the belief that this was a little more than he had counted on."

CHAPTER THIRTEEN

"Seventeen Full Moons"

ONE AUGUST EVENING in 1926, Hughie was out late, as usual, and found himself mixed up in a Broad Street scuffle with an officer of the law named Charles Dean. According to the patrolman's report, at two o'clock in the morning at the corner of Broad and Cypress, Mr. McLoon and another gentleman were embroiled in an animated discussion with two men and two women who were sitting in an idling car.

"Dean in passing heard loud noises." Then, reported the Camden *Courier*, "McLoon and the other three men jumped on the policeman, took his badge, revolver, and keys away, and gave him a beating. McLoon was arrested a square away. Dean identified him."

McLoon was charged with "larceny of club and badge" and "battery of an officer." Dawn found him stewing in the lockup at Seventh and Carpenter.

It was all a mistake. He had played no active role in the defrocking and disarming of Constable Dean, he insisted. The charges were dismissed.

* * *

A month later, Hughie stood at ring center, in a drowning rain, in the light of "157 floodlights, the equivalent of seventeen full moons," before a crowd so enormous and aroused "that you could hear a skyscraper drop," and so hungry "that the hot dogs, if placed end to end, would spell the name of the next Polish prime minister."

In a horseshoe of concrete and concentrated flesh, 127,000 people had come to watch Hughie's buddy Jack Dempsey defend his heavyweight crown for the first time in more than three years. It was stifling for September in the swamplands south of Packer Avenue. The downpour was "God's justice on a sordid affair," smirked the city's killjoys.

The most corrupt and most contented of American metropolises was "demonstrating to the sporting world that it could handle the greatest throng in the sports history of the nation with less confusion than any crowd was ever handled in this country before."

The streetcars ran faultlessly. Ticket scalpers cried for trade. Lemonade costs 25 cents per glass. The sodden sky was filled with "air fanatics, doing the loop-the-loop." A big fight, Philadelphia could manage. A fair election, not so much.

"You saw bankers, lawyers, politicians, porch climbers, physicians, gunmen, small-town comedians, big-city manipulators, small fry, big fry, actors, horse-shoers, tight rope walkers, carpenters and joiners, Channel swim aspirants, three-card monte men, shell workers, ministers' sons, clubmen and persons from every walk, avenue, and boulevard of life," the *Philadelphia Inquirer's* James Isaminger delighted. "If Jack Dempsey was some scrapper before . . . his fame was doubled and quadrupled until it became quite apparent that Goliath was a ham-and-egger."

Less than five feet tall with his seventh- or eighth-grade education, Hughie was right there on the rosined canvas, seen and known by the fevered hundred thousand, carrying the signs that announced the number of the three-minute round to follow. The round card was "bigger than he is," they laughed, a familiar, if unkind, jibe.

It was estimated that one out of every five spectators at the stadium was female: "Flapper and matron, diamond-bedecked movie queen, housewife and business woman, seamstress and Sunday school teacher failed to faint," the *Inquirer*'s reporter smirked:

> They refused to place their hands over their eyes at the sight of the leather-fisted gladiators smashing each other around the ring. ".". Instead they puffed casually at cigarettes; leaned eagerly forward to see every move of the leather-pushers, and cheered wildly as a fighter reeled against the ropes and slumped to the padded floor. Never before in the history of pugilism has the spotlight played upon such a brilliant host of women. . .

The girls were voters, drinkers, renegades, the vanguard of the feminist revolution to come. They were the survivors of the "influ" and the Eddystone explosion. They were the shirtwaist girls who dared to strike in 1910, the sisters of the men who died in the First World War, and the mothers of the men who will fight the Second. They were the finger-snapping flappers who rushed to the rooftops to escape the cops at Spruce and Twenty-Fourth.

"For the millions more who listened in at communal outposts across America, though separated by many miles and divided by ethnic, religious, and psychic differences, it is a civic spectacle at which it means something to be present," wrote Bruce J. Evensen in a book on the great event.[29] He discerned "a newly emerging leisure

---

29 Evensen, Bruce J., *When Dempsey Fought Tunney: Heroes, Hokum and Storytelling in the Jazz Age* (Knoxville, University of Tennessee Press, 1996)

class, nervous for heroic figures to stand above the leveled landscape of industrial living: "That was why so much could be implied by and appeared at risk in Dempsey's return to the ring, a struggle that could be shaped to absorb the attention of thirty-nine million listeners, the largest number of Americans to ever simultaneously witness the same event in the country's history."

In past bouts, Dempsey had disposed of the "Pottawatomie Giant," Jess Willard; the suave Frenchman Carpentier; and Luís Angel Firpo, the "Wild Bull of the Pampas." Now, at the epicenter of South Philly's coliseum, his challenger was James Joseph "Gene" Tunney, "the Fighting Marine," a first-generation Irish-American and former AEF inter-service champion. The urbane antithesis of the ruthless, black-browed Dempsey, Tunney was a blue-eyed New Yorker with James Dean hair, and a reputation as a Greenwich Village *literatus*. A little later in life, he would count George Bernard Shaw as a close friend. The journalists who swarmed Tunney's training camp found him engrossed in Samuel Butler's *The Way of All Flesh* and mocked his erudition.

"I'll knock the big bookworm out inside of eight rounds," was the prediction put into the champion's mouth. Dempsey was a nose-breaker, not a Nostradamus.

From start to finish, in the glare and the rain and the roar, the night was Tunney's. "Time and again Tunney shook Dempsey until the latter's knees bent not with one blow but with a perfect storm of punches. A weaker man, a man with less down-right courage would have surely gone down beneath Tunney's blows. The champion, however, is not of that ilk."

By the time that Hughie McLoon announced the eighth round, the soon-to-be-ex-champion's plastic surgeon was seeing dollar signs: "Dr. William E. Balsinger of Hollywood, Calif., the noted revamper of screen noses, shouted advice to Dempsey, whose nose he recently remodeled . . . The doctor made a mad rush for Dempsey's dressing room in the eighth round, when Tunney socked the champion with a left hand square on the rejuvenated beezer, probably to prepare his tools for immediate action."

Round Ten: "There in that oasis of white in a sea of yelling, frantic spectators gone mad with the spectacle before them, forgetful of the pouring rain that saturated them, Tunney gave the last final proof of his fitness to wear the heavyweight crown.

"Jack's face was a bloody smear, his left eye closed, over his right eye, a gaping wound that he had received earlier in the fray . . . but here was a Dempsey who was still fighting back, feebly it is true, when the bell rang out the tidings of a new champion."

A sanguinary beating under the Queensberry Rules by a United States Marine erased the stain on the slacker's manhood. Two years later, on August 9, 1928, after defeating Dempsey again in the famous "long count" bout in Chicago, Gene Tunney announced publicly that he would marry a millionaire's daughter. Soon they would wed, cross the Atlantic, and lunch in London with Charlotte and George Bernard Shaw.

* * *

Hughie, by 1926, was manager and matchmaker for a passel of mid-range boxers, earning a cut of their purses. One of his charges was Eddie "the Kid" Wagner, another Jewish lightweight out of Philadelphia. Eddie was an intellectual sort, known to spend evenings back home with the actor, playwright, broadcaster, and Communist Clifford Odets at the Horn and Hardart Automat on Broad Street. Hughie, apparently for the first and last time in his life, went west over Christmas, taking the Kid with him.

In San Francisco, Hughie got Wagner a match against a "colored sensation" and "kingpin lightweight of the West" named Jack Thompson, but Eddie had to cancel because of a cut over his eye.

The Kid won a couple of decisions in Hollywood, then traveled back up the coast to face the well-regarded Tommy Cello at the Golden Gate Arena. He lost a ten-round decision.

In April, McLoon steamed back east with his cauliflorists, high-profile enough as a boxing authority to be interviewed by sportswriters when his train paused at Albuquerque. ("Hughy handles a string of two or three leather pushers," said the Albuquerque *Journal*.)

While the leather pushers were on the Pacific shore, a full-page ad appeared in boxing magazine *The Ring* with Eddie (Kid) Wagner's photo on it, along with five other fighters and a bow-tied, older gentleman. "Christmas and New Year's Greetings from Manager Max (Boo Boo) Hoff and his Famous Fighters: Real Fighting Aces: Always Makes Good."

The advertisement gave Boo Boo Hoff's business address in the Banker's Trust Building on Walnut Street in Philadelphia. It also suggested that Boo Boo was the real money behind Eddie Wagner, and Hughie merely the guy who accompanied the boxer for his work on the West Coast. In any event, there can be little doubt that Hoff and McLoon were more than casually acquainted from soirées at the Piccadilly. What the ad did not disclose was Hoff's covert status as the wealthiest, cleverest, and most ruthless bootlegger in the beeriest, crookedest city between the Golden Gate and Delaware Bay.

For the shy and impeccable Hoff, once a teenaged pool room bookie, Prohibition offered the perfect challenge for a brilliant mind. Managing and promoting professional boxers was his public face, but becoming the Andrew Carnegie of organized crime in Pennsylvania was Boo Boo's true calling. During the first decade of mandatory temperance, he would distill, bottle, and distribute illicit liquor by the carload lot, pay off Philadelphia cops and politicians to the tune of two million bucks a year, launder tens of millions of dollars through his own marble-fronted bank, manage a roster of teamsters, accountants, and machine-gunners-for-hire, and avoid publicity, prison, and getting shot.[30]

In 1927, the city was Hoff's. He and his cronies owned the Piccadilly, among other havens for the parched. Billy Sunday would label his kind "a dirty, crooked, sinning, lawless booze gangster," and be right. But if Philadelphians had known who really was behind the Joe-sent-me speakeasies and the pharmacies with the fifths of "medicine" hidden under the counter, they would have called Boo Boo a crafty merchant filling a public demand, even if the "fine Scotch whiskey" he bestowed on them really was little more than lighter fluid tinted with shoe polish, and flavored with a kiss of turpentine.

"Hoff and his associates ran a vertical enterprise," writes Daniel Okrent in *Last Call: The Rise and Fall of Prohibition*, "beginning with the manufacture of alcohol, then managing its diversion to cover houses, its reformulation and repackaging as liquor in a cutting plant, and its wholesale distribution. Hoff and his confederates produced almost 1.5 gallons of undiluted alcohol in a single year—diluted to 80 proof, 3.375 million gallons of regular-strength booze."[31]

According to Hoff's biographer Parry Desmond, when the sour mash hit the fan much later and a grand jury began to peel back the clandestine clockwork of the Hoff empire, "nearly half of the precinct commanders . . . couldn't explain how they could afford such sharp increases in their bank accounts and real estate and stock holdings. One said he had made $7,000 in two years playing craps

---

30 Hoff would die in his own bed in 1941 and leave an estate of one hundred dollars in Bell Telephone stock. The cause of his expiration was listed as "heart ailment," and although murder and suicide both were suspected (there was an empty bottle of sleeping pills by his bed) the real assassin was the repeal of Prohibition. His last business was a milk bar near the Drexel University campus called the Village Barn, a charter member of the Irony Hall of Fame.

31 Okrent, Daniel, *Last Call: The Rise and Fall of Prohibition* (New York, Scribner, 2010).

in the Navy, and another said he generated thousands of dollars by raising canaries."

A photo of Hoff shows the bootlegger, in his trademark bow tie and boater, standing a full foot shorter than a quartet of his light and middleweight fighters. "Boo Boo never smoked or drank," writes Desmond. "His idea of fun at parties was to shoot tiny tinfoil pellets at guests with a rubber band."

Philadelphia folklore holds that Boo Boo never served a day in prison, which is not exactly true. Hoff passed about a week of confinement in York, Pennsylvania, while waiting for bail to be obtained by his favorite lawyer, Congressman Ben Golder.[32] Boo Boo also voluntarily entered the forbidding brick walls of Eastern State Penitentiary once, in 1929, to visit a friend and ally with whom he had just completed an agreement to divide the eastern United States into exclusive fiefs. The deal had been reached at a convocation of killers in Atlantic City. Changing trains in Philadelphia on the way back to Chicago, one of the conventioneers, a certain Alphonse "Scarface" Capone, was nipped for carrying a concealed weapon. He was brought before the Dancing Judge, who imposed bail of $35,000. "I wish it was $100,000," said Magistrate Carney. "I believe you are responsible for many murders."

Capone, whose territory was actually smaller than Hoff's, hired Rep. Golder as his defense counsel. The scene shifted to Municipal Court and a higher-ranking judge. "Magistrate Edward P. Carney— white carnation and all—was called to the stand," the *Inquirer* reported, "and asked what happened when Capone and his gun-carrying bodyguard, 'Slippery Frankie Rio,' was arrested as he was leaving a movie theater at Nineteenth and Market Streets."

---

32 Hoff was acquitted of all charges when, near the end of his life, he shot an old schoolmate and close friend in both calves for failing to fully pay back a loan.

"Have you any proof that Mr. Capone is a murderer?" demanded Golder. "You fixed bail . . . to keep him in jail."

"Well, that's about the size of it," retorted Carney. "Philadelphia is not afraid of you, Al Capone, and I'm not afraid of you."

* * *

In 1927, Hughie McLoon's problem was not Al Capone: it was that nobody was afraid of "Lanky" Ralph Smith, a fighter he had picked up out west. A former fireman and a sparring partner for Jack Dempsey, the heavyweight Smith, standing close to six feet, six inches tall, was the biggest thing that happened to Hughie in the remaining months of his brief existence. The papers had a field day with the altitudinal differential between manager and fighter.

After a few warm-up bouts against Jack "Manslaughter" Rozier, Hughie gauged Lanky Smith's limits and turned down $5000 to fight the promising African American, George Godfrey. He accepted instead $750 for a bout with the less-terrifying and operatically named Roberto Roberti. Lanky got laid out anyway.

Now the manager had to make the walk of shame to all the newspapers to convince the pugilistic cosmos that Lanky still had the right stuff. Hughie was at the zenith of wise-guy fame:

Says Hughey McLoon, the smallest fight manager in the world, "Well, mebbe Ralph Smith can't lick George Godfrey and Roberto Roberti, but he sure can smear the rest of these bums."

Ralph, who is as tall as Hughey is short, has been handing out nothing but kayoes since he recovered from the beating the young Eyetalian giant handed him in our arena. Last week, he finished Gene Jeannette, of Norristown, in the second round of the windup in Gene's home town. Smith outweighed the colored boy by 33 pounds. . .

Lanky Ralph Smith never would make a lasting mark on the heavy-weight rankings. By the summer of 1928, he was working as a sparring partner and lucky Hughie was realizing that if he kept relying on the sweet science for his sustenance, his future was bleak.

* * *

For his twenty-sixth birthday on July 21, 1928, Elizabeth Palmer McLoon Geatens bought her first-born son a new watch, the Waltham that he won at Our Lady of Mount Carmel School having stopped ticking after eighteen years. In return, Hughie brought a canary to his mom's new residence at 1508 Shunk Street. The bird was "to keep me and Danny company," Elizabeth said. Danny was Hughie's half-brother, aged ten. Half-sister Dorothy was twenty-one and married. Peter Geatens, Hughie's stepfather, was unmentioned.

Hughie slid into the hospitality industry on Cuthbert Street. Whether Max Hoff grubstaked him to be a purveyor of his brands or whether another Ralph, (whose last name kept changing in the newspapers,) paid the freight,[33] "Ralph and Hughey's Café," at 927 Cuthbert Street, was bustling by mid-July. It was not the Ritz-Carlton or the Bellevue-Stratford. It was located on a minor street in a three-story building that had seen many uses over the years. In 1903, "candy, chewing gum, and Spanish peanut vending penny machines, all metal," were manufactured there. "Have your piano tuned for $1, Postal 927 Cuthbert," read an ad from 1916.

Ralph and Hughey's was far from the only speakeasy in Philadelphia in the summer of 1928 but it was busy enough that it was regularly raided by the honorable Philly police. There was even a report that there was a warrant for Hughie's arrest as a violator of

---

33 Most people called the co-owner Ralph Maloney, even though he claimed his real name was Pennock. "I have no idea why they call me Maloney," Maloney said.

Prohibition, which may have meant that he and Ralph had not been paying enough to Boo Boo's boys for protection.

On July 14, "dry agents" came around to 927 Cuthbert and purchased "several drinks of alleged whisky." Their researches yielded "fifteen quarts of liquor, a like amount of champagne." A week later, federal G-men discovered "two barrels of beer testing more than 3 per cent alcohol" in a rear room. It would have been bigger news if Hughie McLoon had not had a hidden pail of pale ale for sale. But somebody had "arrest Hughie" on a to-do list. On July 22, the G-men returned. "More than a score of patrons were startled when the agents vaulted the bar," noted the *Inquirer*, drily.

CHAPTER FOURTEEN

The Glazed Eye
Of Death

RANCOCAS CREEK IS A SLOW, mussy stream that rises in the Pine Barrens of southern New Jersey, makes a parenthetical turn at Delanco and enters the Delaware River between Philadelphia and Trenton. In the 1920s, the quiet north bank of the Rancocas was "the recreation ground of the racketeers," the place where "the shock troops of gangdom rested from the street battles of Philadelphia."

There, in a little cottage, two girls named Jennie and Doris, or Mary and Grace (undoubtedly aliases), "entertained during the dull days from Monday to Friday while the gunmen were resting from the weekend assaults on the city":

The four-room house sat in the woods bordering the creek. It was furnished like a barracks with cots, a few chairs, and a stove. Names such as "Dan," "Doris," and "Joe" were carved in the woodwork. A sign on the door read "Pres. Burns of the Racket Club." It didn't mean tennis.

There was a gravel pit about fifty yards from the bunkhouse. The excavation of sand and aggregates has been an important industry along the Rancocas since the eighteenth century. But from 1920 to 1933, with illegal alcoholic beverages overtaking excavation as a local mine of wealth, speedboats and barges laden with French champagne, Canadian rye, and Boo Boo Hoff's juniper-flavored kerosene snuck up the Delaware, turned right at Riverside, New Jersey, and disappeared into the shadowed glades.

Evidence suggests that it was in the little cottage in the Jersey woods, on a sleepless summer night in early August 1928, that four men and two women storyboarded the murder of Hughie McLoon.

"The gangsters spent their time in the country practicing shooting," the Phildelphia *Record* reported, when the hideaway was discovered and its denizens were either dead or on trial. "The trees about the cottage were scarred by bullets. One big oak apparently represented a man standing on the sidewalk, for a short distance away a chair was placed to represent the back seat of an automobile. The oak was riddled with high-powered bullets of the sort that pierced the body of McLoon on Cuthbert Street.

"The racketeers did not make friends with the country folk."

* * *

The timeline of the first two weeks of August 1928 is muddy as the river, silted with the denials and dubious alibis of the accused, churned by the over-eager guesses of a dozen competing newspapers, and dammed by the fact that the only man who knew the truth was shot to pieces and buried at Holy Cross.

Blending the conflicting and sensationalized newspaper accounts with sworn testimony from the courts may not generate enough pure truth to satiate Bertrand Russell, but it is all we have.

On Saturday, August 4, 1928, there was a night of dancing in Philadelphia attended by "Doris Kearns," her roommate "Mary Gilbert," and Hughie McLoon, who was taking a break from the café he had been operating with Ralph Pennock for a scant two weeks (or five months, depending on your newspaper.)

The location is uncertain. It may have been a ten-cents-a-tango palladium, a "dry" hotel ballroom, or a private party. Or it may have been the infamous "high class vice resort" operated by an entrepreneur named Rose Hicks at the intercourse of Thirteenth and Master Streets, where Hughie might have been enjoying some lay-by time with one of his pals from the boxing world. Doris Kearns may have been a member of the labor force at the Hicks establishment.

Wherever it happened, according to investigators, Hughie, "in his normal role a laughing, witty, clever youngster; in his cups often quarrelsome," made a pass at Doris Kearns. Or at Mary Gilbert. Or at both. Although some still saw him as a child, he was a man of twenty-six with a man's desires, and a man's dreams. The moll (whichever it was) looked down and laughed at the humpback's impudence, mocked his deformity, and vowed to tell her boyfriend.

In some accounts, the woman's beau was Samuel Grossman, a Callowhill Street motorcar mechanic, garage owner, and purveyor of high-powered "big machines" to the drive-by-murder trade. Thus from a Camden paper:

> Miss Mary Gilbert, said to be a friend of Grossman's, was taken from her rooms on Jefferson Street near Broad this morning and quizzed at headquarters. Detectives had heard that she had been forced to receive the attentions of McLoon, and then had told Grossman of her insult.

In other reports, the woman who rebuffed Hughie's advances was Doris Kearns and the vengeful paramour was the amoral but devastatingly attractive Danny O'Leary, the longshoreman's son from South Philly. They may have been the "Dan" and "Doris" carved into the door at Rancocas Creek.

In 1927, O'Leary was brought before the carnation of Magistrate Edward P. Carney on a charge of "being concerned in a $14,000 payroll holdup," but the Dancing Judge sent him home to his wife and their baby for lack of evidence. O'Leary also had been accused in 1925 of shooting a policeman in Camden, and in May 1928, he was booked for "highway robbery," but both of those charges were dropped as well.

Either way, Hughie's good fortune was running out. In daring to imagine himself in the arms of a whole man's woman, he had gone too far. He had tried to climb through the one-way glass into a world able to see him only as a freak. For nearly twenty years, in his tiny mascot Mummer's parade through the streets and dugouts and prize rings of Philadelphia, McLoon had dusted off the degradation, accepted the body that the seesaw gave him, and grinned his way to fame. But never had there been an insult like this and it got the better of him.

Later that night or very early the next day, McLoon accosted "Doris Kearns," variously described as a "beautiful blonde," "a tall girl, about twenty-five," and a "mysterious beauty queen of the underworld," in her flat at 1409 Jefferson Street. He revealed how deeply her derision had wounded him, trashed the apartment, and whacked her on the beezer.

(In the Philadelphia *Evening Bulletin*'s version of events, McLoon slapped Doris in the face while they still were at the dance when she made fun of his hump. When he returned to his Cuthbert Street café, Hughie told Billy Meister about the fracas and "the latter got him further incensed." They went to the apartment in which she lived with Mary Gilbert and broke up the furniture. McLoon gave Doris a black eye.)

While this was happening at 1409 Jefferson, on this same summer Saturday, Samuel Grossman, Samuel A. "Shorty" Feldman, and Francis Peterson decided to take a motor trip to New Jersey "for corn," according to Grossman's testimony a week later.

"When we came back," Grossman said, "we went to McLoon's saloon and talked to him. I wanted to know why he hit my girl and gave her a black eye."

At Ralph and Hughey's, the three men were confronted by Meister and Fries. "They wanted to put on a gun fight then and there," Grossman contended, but his side was short of bullets and let it go.

A few days later, at seven o'clock on the morning of Wednesday, August 8, someone rang the bell at Doris and Mary's place on Jefferson.

"Two men came to her apartment and asked for Samuel Grossman's telephone number," Kearns related. She was not inclined to provide it but when one of the visitors "made a move as though to produce a gun," she coughed up the number. As the two men left, they instructed Ms. Kearns to tell Mr. Grossman that Dan and Shorty were there.

On that warm Wednesday evening, just before heading over to Cuthbert Street to serve "light lunch" and ladle tepid beer and Boo Boo's booze, Hughie visited Magistrate Carney at his suite.

"I guess it was just about 9:45 at night that he dropped in," Carney related the next day.

"I suggested that we take a ride to Atlantic City. He said he didn't want to go, however, and then made a strange remark. 'I guess this will be my last night over at Cuthbert Street. I'm getting tired of it. I'm going to get out of there.'

"I don't know whether it was a hunch or not," said the Dancing Judge, too weary and grieving to measure the words he chose, "but it looks as though Hugh foresaw something. He has been a good, clean-living boy always. He was the idol of his mother."

"That boy was not mixed up in any so-called 'rackets,'" Edward Carney averred. "I am thoroughly convinced because I have taken a personal interest in him for several years and he was a daily caller at my rooms at the Sylvania Hotel."

Moonshine made strange bedfellows. On the evening of August 8, even after everything that had happened at the dance and at 1409 Jefferson, Doris Kearns and Mary Gilbert went out with Meister and Fries for a night on the town. One of their stops was a joint called "the G. & G.," at the corner of Girard and Germantown.

What happened next was reported by the *Evening Bulletin*, quoting testimony by Charles Beckman, Captain of Detectives. It may be the closest thing we have to what actually occurred that night. Beckman picked up the timeline at the G. & G:

> While they were there, Grossman, O'Leary, Feldman, and Peterson entered the place. Meister, Fries, and the two women left by a side door and jumped into Fries' automobile. The four others followed them, with Grossman driving.
>
> Meister and Fries took the women to their apartment. On the way, Fries said to the women, "Keep down, they're after us and they may shoot." They got the women home safely, and then went to McLoon's place.

"When McLoon saw them he got nervous," said Beckman. It seems that Meister and Fries, on the one hand, and O'Leary, Feldman, Grossman, and Peterson on the other, had quarreled in Hughie's establishment the previous Saturday. "The fuss about the girl had something to do with that also. Anyhow, when Meister and Fries told [Hughie] that the others had been gunning for them, McLoon said, 'Well, get out of here. I don't want any more rows in this place. If you don't get out I'll close up.'"

Edward P. Carney: "Hugh tried to be diplomatic with the fellows and joshed them out as far as the entrance to the place, patting them on the back and telling them not to disturb the neighborhood. When they reached the corner they were apparently convinced that it would be unfair to start any rowdyism and from what I understand McLoon was just leaving them when the murder car came by."

* * *

Events played out just as they had been practiced on the big oak tree on the creekside in New Jersey. "Duck, quick!" Fries was said to have shouted as the murder car came near. He jumped one way, Meister another. McLoon, frozen, took the brunt of the attack.

As soon as the gunfire ceased, thirty-three-year-old Virginia Fineman, *née* Morozzi, the girl from the stub end of Leithgow Street who used to push little Hughie's pram, and who was now "checking coats" on the second floor of Hughie's eatery on that stifling August night, came vaulting down to the sidewalk and discovered her boss, the popular hunchback and sportsman-about-town, crumpled on the shoe-shop stairway. She saw Meister and Fries, the familiar thugs (and, a minute earlier, customers), trying to squirm away toward safety, and noticed that somebody's pistol had been discarded or dropped on the pavement a few feet away.

The firemen from Engine Company 20 weren't even there yet when Ralph Pennock came running into the café and shouted: "O'Leary and Feldman and Peterson shot Hughie!"

Virginia Fineman called Magistrate Carney at the Sylvania Hotel, and repeated what she heard from Ralph Pennock.

A week later, Mrs. Fineman, "who broke under stress after disappearing from the ken of the police," would race screaming through the buffed stone vaults of City Hall ("her shrieks echoed and re-echoed down the corridors"), wailing and bawling that she had never said it was anyone but O'Leary—she had never mentioned Shorty Feldman or Francis Peterson—it was only O'Leary, Danny O'Leary, who shot Hughie McLoon from the window of the big, black car.

"Are you afraid?" she would be asked on the witness stand, after denying that she heard Pennock's announcement, because there were "twenty or forty people in the place" and it was too noisy to hear anything, even gunshots.

"No."

But on the night of the murder, Magistrate Carney would swear under oath, Virginia Morozzi Fineman fingered all three men, almost as if she had known what was coming before it happened, as if she had known who would be in that black machine that Sammy Grossman was driving, as if she had known whose short but storied life they were out to end.

Someone had to know when Meister and Fries were exiting McLoon's place. As for Pennock, he claimed that he just happened to be heading out for some fresh air when the "big motor" hauled up and the hurricane of hot lead flew. He showed off a slight wound, or a powder burn, on one hand, but when the trials began a couple of weeks later and everybody else started denying everything, Pennock changed his story, too, and laughed and lied: "My girlfriend scratched me."

By 2:00 a.m., "a few shattered bits of glass from an automobile windshield, a tight-lipped material witness who knows but refuses to name the murderers, and a maze of conflicting theories confronted perplexed police."

"More than four vehicles full of gunmen started out after McLoon was pronounced dead, seeking vengeance," reported the Camden *Times*. "Heavily armed police and sleuths are touring the city to prevent further bloodshed."

"McLoon, a hunchback, was a familiar figure in the sporting world."

As if the city didn't know.

* * *

A fireman named Toner testified that he was among the first to reach the wounded men. He and a colleague named Hefferman were on duty that night at Engine Company 20 on Commerce Street.

They heard a sharp shot and, after a brief silence, two roars. They ran to Tenth Street on time to see the big black sedan, its driver bent over the steering wheel as he turned the corner. Two men were in the back seat. The firemen were unable to see their faces.

"Fries was hobbling about the street while Meister was sprawled on the sidewalk moaning," said Toner. "At first we thought they were the only ones hurt and while we were helping them into Fries' car, which was riddled, we heard of McLoon."

Joseph Fries was rather an expert at this sort of thing. Just six weeks earlier, on June 29, he had been wounded in the neck during a shootout at Race and Franklin Streets.

On the northeast corner, Toner continued, the firemen saw a flight of eight steps leading to the basement shoe shop of R.C.D. Devine. McLoon had apparently staggered to the top of the steps and fallen unconscious to the bottom.

Fries, although injured, insisted that he drive to the hospital. The firemen heaped McLoon into the rear seat and, hearing their alarm bell from the station, ran off to answer it, leaving the sidewalk and the stairway wet with blood.

* * *

Hughie was still alive when they got him to Jefferson Hospital. It was three o'clock in the morning. The night staff assayed the condition of the famous little man. He had been shot once through the right eye. Three more bullets had struck the side of his face. Others hit his right arm, his chest, and his feet.

Magistrate Carney was one of the first to Hughie's bedside. He arrived at the infirmary within minutes of Virginia Fineman's call.

He told the swarming reporters that the victim had been on his staff for a time in the mid-twenties, processing paperwork, copying files, hanging around city hall. "Mcloon had nothing," he said. "He was just about making a living out of his café and cabaret."

The *Inquirer* confirmed that Hughie had nothing. Notwithstanding his "spectacular career," and whatever else was going on behind the bar and upstairs at Ralph and Hughey's at 927 Cuthbert, the hunchback's investment portfolio on the night he was slaughtered amounted to a quarter of a dollar.

Outside of Jefferson Hospital, a crowd of two hundred people, many of them in evening clothes, most of whom claiming to be friends of the victim, gathered and made anxious inquiries." Inside, a night-shift priest from the Church of St. John the Evangelist performed the last rites, praying away Philadelphia's most popular little scholar of the year 1910.

"McLoon never regained consciousness," the Dancing Judge sighed.

Hughie's friends wept and swore in the accident ward when told he was dead.

* * *

There was little time for grieving with killers on the loose. The magistrate "took an ante-mortem statement from Meister, notified McLoon's mother of what had occurred, and hurried away to make a private investigation into the shooting."

A police bulletin called for the arrest of two gangsters, Grossman and Feldman, said to be well known to the authorities. The pair were considered violent enemies of Meister and Fries, and the two sides "were thought to have agreed to shoot out their differences."

The initial investigation convinced police that McLoon had not been the target of the murderers. He had simply been in unlucky company. For the first time in several years of violence, there was no round-up of suspects following the shooting,

The crime scene surrendered only one definite clue, and not a great one at that. Shattered glass, apparently from a broken window or the headlight of the gangsters' car, was found in the street. Police kept a lookout for an automobile missing a light or windshield.

McLoon's mother arrived at the hospital and collapsed when she saw his body. It was not necessary for her to lift the sheet from his face to know it was her son," said one report, "as the white gold wrist watch she had presented him recently was on his arm."

* * *

In September, at Congregation Beth Shalom at the corner of Broad and Courtland Streets, with Sammy Grossman and Shorty Feldman in custody for the murder of Hughie McLoon, Rabbi Mortimer J. Cohen delivered a sermon that he titled "The Shame of Israel."

"Rarely has a portion of the Jewish people sunk to such depths as some of our people in this city," the rabbi began.

> "There is no pardoning the lawlessness and the violation of every canon of human decency; above all there is no pardoning the taking of human life.
>
> What a shame has come to Israel in the crimes of a lawless few! What disgrace is ours through these men, less than human, who have dragged the Jewish name through the mud and filth of murder and bribery and corruption.
>
> In a sense every man and woman who uses the forbidden is as guilty of the crimes as these men . . . in every glass of hard drink there is mixed the blood of the victims, and out of every cup

there peers the glazed eye of death that we have made possible by our willingness to purchase what these men sell.

All in this whole City of Philadelphia, 'we have sinned, O God, all of us together; we have sinned!"

CHAPTER FIFTEEN

"Before You Leave"

THE GRINNING BAT BOY'S final inning was a gathering of conspicuous grief on the morning of Monday, August 13, 1928, on Shunk Street in South Philadelphia. Hughie was enthroned in his casket with the wreath that spelled "Idol" as his crown. The canary was silent, its cage covered with a cloth.

"The poor bird wonders what's the matter," Hughie's mother cried. "Oh, if my son had only stayed home last night!"

The woman, sobbing so violently she could no longer speak, collapsed onto the sofa.

"Before you leave," she pleaded to her first-born when she recovered her breath, "I am asking God to forgive the men who harmed you!"

Two thousand neighbors, silent, their heads bare, eyed the silver casket as it descended the narrow steps. Above them, filling the two-story dwelling, were floral tributes from Connie Mack, Boo Boo Hoff, boardwalk emperor Mickey Duffy, saloonkeeper Texas

Guinan, bandleader Ted Lewis, actors, comedians, athletes, officials, strangers. There were so many garlands, horseshoes, bouquets, and circles of orchids that it required "three large touring cars to transport them to the cemetery."

Hoff promised $1,500 from his meager earnings as a boxing promoter for the send-off, and a gift of $2,500 for the pious, wailing mother. The Dancing Judge, without his carnation, without his godson, said he would match the sum.

Not a single report noted the presence (or absence) of Peter Geatens, Hughie's stepfather, legal or otherwise, since the lad was five. A few days later, there would be a photo in the newspaper with Peter in a bow tie, looking calm and complacent, standing behind his tortured wife, their daughter Dorothy, Elizabeth's sister, and Eddie Carney, his blossom back in place.

Another thousand citizens knelt at St. Monica's for Hughie's liturgical farewell. Then came the slow procession to Yeadon, flanked by six police cars carrying members of the murder squad. An armored vehicle with bullet proof glass contained another officer, three burly guards, and a chauffeur who was armed in case of emergency. Detectives mingled with the crowd, looking for suspects who may have been involved in the murder. None were recognized.

The underworld, said the *Philadelphia Bulletin*, was "reported seething over the latest outbreak of gang warfare."

"Whether or not there is a measure of public service in the riddance from the community of some of its undesirables through 'gang warfare,'" the paper said, "it is a frightful condition in any city. Hughie McLoon does not appear to have been the target of the gangsters' guns, but not infrequently when the sawed-off shotguns and machine guns begin to play in the city streets other citizens even less acquainted with the gangs than was McLoon are victims."

The commentary was vicious, but true. Like his old pal Stuffy McInnis, Hughie had been playing too close to the foul line.

At Holy Cross, grave diggers in blue overalls closed the lid on Hughie's $1,500 oak coffin. His mother pulled the veil from her face. "That's my darling boy," she moaned. "Oh my! Oh my!"

The papers acknowledged "something beyond ordinary devotion between Hughie and his mother." The accident that had broken his back had brought them closer together. Hughie had been all she'd had, and for seven years she had nursed him back onto his feet. She dropped a white aster into the grave and sobbed.

That same Monday afternoon, up on West Lehigh Avenue, with fifteen thousand people in the Shibe Park stands and hundreds more cheering from the rooftops, the Athletics jumped out to a 2–0, first-inning lead over the Detroit Tigers on a single, a double, a groundout, and a sacrifice fly. Those were all the runs that Robert Moses "Lefty" Grove needed. He allowed only a pair of singles in a 7–1 victory, his seventeenth win of the year. The Mackmen, with seven future hall-of-famers in the lineup, even worked a steal of home plate, baseball's most thrilling play.

Barren of championships since the death of Louis Van Zelst in March 1915, and a slapstick act during and after McLoon's three seasons as mascot, they were once again on the verge of great things, and still under the management of Connie Mack, now aged sixty-five. The next season, the Athletics would claim the first of three consecutive American league pennants. Their long jinx was over.

Hughie McLoon missed a hell of a game.

* * *

In the days following the murder, Danny O'Leary was seen to "drink heavily and do a lot of talking in saloons," vowing intemperately that, "If I take a fall, I ain't taking the 'rap' alone."

On Tuesday, August 14, Danny told his latest young, pretty, black-haired lover—"a wise girl with wide lips"—that he wanted to go to New

Jersey to escape the heat. They were in a flat at 1826 North Park Avenue in Philadelphia, which the girl had rented while pretending to be the wife of a certain Joey Burns—perhaps the same man whose name was knife-etched at Rancocas as "Pres. Burns of the Racket Club."

Outside the Park Avenue house, according to the young woman, who went by the name of Jennie Brooks and who would be known for the rest of her life as "the decoy girl," Danny O'Leary encountered Francis Peterson and Shorty Feldman: "They were looking for him to tell him he was in danger of being bumped off."

"I ain't afraid of none of 'em," pretty Danny snarled.

Heading to Camden over the two-year-old Ben Franklin Bridge, and then north on White Horse Pike, Danny and Jennie realized that their cab was being followed by "a large touring car" with four or five men inside.

At a Garden State tavern, the men from the big touring car tried to pick a fight with O'Leary, but "Danny was so drunk the other fellows at the bar always stopped it." The girlfriend called for a hack to haul her heartthrob back to North Park Avenue. The cab driver had to carry Danny upstairs as he babbled drunkenly about the fellows in the touring car. Said Jennie in her subsequent testimony:

> I judge we were asleep about half to three-quarters of an hour when I was awakened by something or somebody. I just can't remember whether someone pulled my arm or whether it was the steady glare of a flashlight which I became aware was being played on my face and on poor Danny's sleeping form.

Jennie's skirt, part of a "pink georgette ensemble," was beside her on the floor.

> Before I could speak, I heard a voice say something and I saw a man's eyes under a cap. Suddenly there came the strangest

hissing sound I ever heard—sist—sist—sist—five times, just like that, and no louder.

It was the hiss of death. I didn't know it then, but I soon discovered they were pumping bullets into Dan's body with one of those silent guns.

Every time the thing hissed it spat out a blue flame.

I waited for a few minutes until I felt they had gone. I jumped up and turned on the electric light and rushed over and shook Dan's shoulder. This caused the blood to flow freely from the wounds in his arm and chest.

I screamed out the first time when I looked down and saw that my hands were full of blood. You see, I really loved Danny and I feel sure that he loved me.

* * *

Danny O'Leary's attractive corpse drew a police detail and almost as big a burial day crowd as Hughie's, but not quite—only about ten thousand fans. Among the floral tributes, said the *Evening Bulletin*, was a wreath from Petey Ford, a gangster serving a sentence of twelve-and-a-half to twenty-five years. Mr. Ford was the mug with whom Hughie McLoon was engaged in conversation on Broad Street on that night in 1926 when Officer Charles Dean's badge and gun got pinched. A year after that, Ford was jailed after he put three slugs into, but failed to finish off, Mickey Duffy, the pseudo-Irish beer baron who was, in fact, a Pole named Cusick.

Jennie Brooks, after ten days of police interrogation, finally admitted to being Mrs. Antonio Marcello, age sixteen, a runaway from a marriage she had entered two years earlier to spite her parents. Before that, she was the schoolgirl Anna Pechler of South Napa Street, a child of "hard-working but poor" Hungarian stock. She had been considered demure and well-behaved.

"I know she is not a decoy girl," Anna's father, Albert, insisted. "She doesn't come from a family that will do things like that."

At first, Signor Marcello, a chauffeur, "took care of me and loved me," his baby signora said of the man she married at the age of fourteen, but he was "stingy" whenever Anna wanted to go out on the town.

"I don't know just how it happened," she confessed to any reporter who asked her:

> . . . But after I met Danny I just couldn't help caring for him. He made me leave my husband and run away with him. You see, we loved each other dearly.
>
> I didn't know that Danny had ever done anything under-handed. I didn't know that his friends were gangsters.
>
> They told me they were business men. Why should I doubt them?

* * *

On the seventeenth of August, on Third Street at Market in a drench-ing rainstorm, stunned businessmen watched as Officer Charlie Brown and two colleagues, guns drawn, flung open the door of a small coupe and wrestled the driver out and onto the puddled pavement.

"Hello, Charlie," said the evacuee. It was Samuel A. "Shorty" Feldman. He and Officer Brown had met before, under similar circumstances.

"I might as well let you take me," Feldman smiled. "If not they'd get me sooner or later anyway, or the dicks would nail me in a year or so."

One killer buried, one in cuffs, two to go.

At 7:30 that evening, Francis Peterson strolled right into Jennie Brooks's apartment on North Park Street and found two police officers waiting for him. The decoy girl was batting a thousand, although it was not always clear which team she was playing for.

"Hold up your hands," ordered a detective named Faries as he pointed his gun at Peterson.

Instead of holding up his hands, Peterson pulled an automatic pistol from a shoulder holster. As he drew, a policeman grabbed him with one hand and with his other brought a blackjack down on the suspect's head. Faries followed up with a blow to Peterson's jaw and a smash in the ribs. Fourteen clips of bullets, six bullets per clip, were found on his person.

Sammy Grossman was an easier capture, snared at his garage. Charles Beckman, the captain of detectives, brought Peterson into the room where Grossman was being held.

"Do you know this man?" Beckman asked.

"I never saw him before," Peterson answered.

"Why you dirty liar," snapped Grossman. "Why don't you tell the truth? You know that you were out with me, that you went down to New Jersey with me, to my place there, together with O'Leary and Feldman. And you know that you were in McLoon's place with O'Leary and Feldman on the Saturday night before McLoon was killed, and you got in a fuss with Meister and Fries there."

"Peterson paled slightly," reported the *Bulletin*. Sammy Grossman was doing a better detective job than Captain Beckman.

"Then Feldman was brought in, and he admitted readily that he knows Grossman. After that Peterson changed his attitude and admitted Grossman's narrative was right. But he said he had known the other men only a short time."

Grossman was charged with suspicion of murder. Feldman was charged with murder and operating a motor vehicle without a license. Peterson was charged with murder, assault and battery upon detectives with intent to kill, and carrying concealed weapons. Jennie Brooks was booked as a "suspicious character."

At 5437 Chestnut Street, on the same day, Mrs. Francis Peterson, "a frail figure in a peach-colored summer dress half-covered by a white apron," stroked the hair of "a grey-eyed boy who, proud of his blue overalls, gave their shoulder strap an important hitch."

"Her large brown eyes were appealing, even if her lips were silent." Finally, the woman spoke. "I'm sticking by him through thick or thin," she said.

On Broad Street, under the hat of William Penn, who perhaps envisioned a less bourbon-drenched, bloodthirsty, lying, murdering colony than Philadelphia turned out to be, Feldman's wife, a diminutive blonde, called at City Hall and tearfully insisted that her husband was innocent of all charges.

"I just know the detectives are wrong," she wept.

* * *

At 9 o'clock in the evening on Saturday, August 18, a twenty-four-year-old man named Jim Daly, just home from a stint as a professional boxer in California, entered a tavern at the corner of Woodstock and Berks Streets that was operated by a couple of cousins named McAtee.

Howard J. McAtee was tending bar when the conversation turned to the demise of Hughie McLoon, who had been dead for a little more than two hundred hours and *in pace* at Holy Cross for half that long.

"Hughie was shot because he was a fresh kid," McAtee said.

"That isn't so," retorted Daly. "Hughie McLoon was as decent a young fellow as they come."

Upset by Daly's defense of McLoon, McAtee took a revolver from his hip pocket and fired a slug into Daly's crotch. As the victim fell to the floor, McAtee reached over the bar and fired another shot into his writhing body. The saloon's patrons fled in horror. Daly somehow got to his feet, stumbled across the floor, and fell out the front door.

Policemen patrolling along Twentieth Street heard the shots and rushed to the scene. They found McAtee behind the bar, "grim and unexcited," waiting to surrender.

When Daly and his assailant arrived at Northwestern General Hospital, Magistrate Edward P. Carney, was already there. Ubiquitous and unafraid of Capones and lesser *capi*, the Dancing Judge had passed a grievous fortnight. He hauled McAtee to Daly's bedside and took a "pre-mortem" statement (the most common kind) from the moaning Daly.

"There's the man who shot me," the batboy's defender said, adding nothing more.

* * *

The *habeus corpus* hearings for Hughie's accused destroyers were vaudeville. It was as if the 1916 Pathetics were running the criminal courts. Ralph Pennock was on the stand:

"Are you afraid to tell who killed McLoon?"

"I don't know anything about it."

"You were there, you showed Judge Carney a bullet mark on your wrist, and you know he saw it. Now you know Judge Carney wouldn't try to frame you. He's too big a man. I think you're afraid of these rats."

"I protest against the reflections on the character of my client," yelped William A. Gray, counsel for Francis Peterson, Sr.

"Objection overruled," gaveled the presiding justice, a man named Edwin O. Lewis. "I don't think language can reflect anything on the character of men engaged or implicated in any way in gang warfare."

"You were in the street, why don't you tell the truth? Didn't you run back inside and yell that Peterson, Grossman, Feldman and O'Leary had just killed Hughie?"

"No, Peterson had never been to that saloon, I don't know that Feldman had ever been there, and as for Grossman, the first time that I ever saw him was when I looked over the prisoners' room."

The redheaded Virginia Morozzi Fineman, born on Christmas Day, 1897, but still "youthful in appearance . . . was smartly dressed in a tan and brown ensemble suit and a brown felt hat. She appeared to be nervous and kept swinging her feet. She spoke hardly above a whisper and Judge Lewis asked her to use her voice."

"I am using it," she replied, "without raising it in the least."

"I went to Magistrate Carney in the Sylvania Hotel after the shooting," she deposed.

"Were you sober?"

"I was sober enough. I don't know what his motive is in saying I told him who did the shooting. It is a lie. Even the next day I didn't know whether I saw the name O'Leary or imagined it."

"You are afraid now?

"No."

"Excited?"

"Yes."

"Do you remember [Pennock] running in after the shooting?"

"Nobody came in."

Joseph Fries took the oath.

"Fries, are you a gangster?" he was asked.

"I object!" a counselor named Werblun protested.

"Overruled!"

Fries: "I'm a carnival man."

"Do you know Grossman?"

"No."

"Come on, you know Grossman. Take a good look at those defendants. You know Grossman and he's here."

"I never saw these men before."

"Whose gun is this?" the prosecutor demanded, brandishing the long-barreled revolver that was jettisoned onto the Cuthbert Street sidewalk that fatal night.

"I don't know. It ain't mine. I never carry a gun."

Firefighter Hefferman, discoverer of the abandoned pistol at the scene of the murder, "started to flourish the weapon around, whereupon lawyers and spectators squirmed to get out of range."

A few weeks later, at a coroner's inquest, Meister and Fries reunited.

"You were shot also?" asked the coroner, Fred Schwartz, Jr.

"Yes, sir, in the left hip," said Meister, who had failed to die of his numerous wounds.

"Where did those shots come from—from the sky? Was there a machine gun up there shooting down at you?"

"All I cared about was that I was shot."

"On which side—the side you carry your gun on?"

After a moment's hesitation, the witness laughed.

"No, where I carry my cigarettes."

Fries was sworn in.

"Why, here is a fellow who stood alongside Hughie McLoon when he was killed," said Coroner Schwartz, "and he won't tell a thing. It's the most ridiculous thing I've ever heard. Do you know who shot McLoon?"

"No."

"Do you know who shot you?"

"No."

"Do you know from which direction you were shot?"

"I didn't want to look."

"You were fond of McLoon?"

"Sure! Everybody was."

* * *

By 1928, it had been a quarter century since Lincoln Steffens had raised Philadelphia's glove in the air as the heavyweight champion of corruption. Now, finally, pitifully, and fruitlessly, the city moved to reject the designation, just as Smedley Darlington Butler once spurned the Medal of Honor.

On August 18, even as he presided over the chimera of the Hughie McLoon death inquiry, Judge Edwin O. Lewis ordered the convening of a special grand jury (including one woman and two African Americans) to unknot the sinews that bound bootleggers, politicians, and police in a tangle of profit and sin.

"A survey yesterday had shown that liquor operations in Philadelphia have assumed flagrant proportions," the *Inquirer* advised on the day the grand jury was announced. "In the center of the city scores of saloons are doing a thriving business with their swinging doors continually swaying under the patronage of thirsty persons."

What emerged the next spring was a portrait of a law-enforcement agency that greedily sucked at the bootleggers' teats, a manufactory of illegal hooch to rival U.S. Steel in synergy and profit with miniature Max Hoff as its CEO, and a population tipsily delighted with the status quo. The carnage in the streets, and the decoy's beds, was the inevitable by-product of wicked men colliding with a ridiculous law.

Wary enough never to sign a document connecting himself with illicit activity, and so famous from his boxing promotions that his sudden subpoena to City Hall in bow tie and boater was a front-page stunner, Boo Boo was as frisky as a featherweight as he began his eight rounds of testimony, and as blood-smeared as ex-champ Dempsey when the last bell rang.

The grand jury concluded:

> That the trafficking of liquor was so important a business that Philadelphia, not to be shamed by Chicago, had for its very own a "King of the Bootleggers." Despite the fact that the Grand Jury

subpoenaed this "boss bootlegger," whom it at various times identified as Max "Boo Boo" Hoff, to testify before it eight times, it was unable to indict him. . . .

Investigation by the Grand Jury brought forth a statement that Captain Beckman, head of the Detectives Bureau, was the possessor of a personal fortune approximating $75,000, the source of which he was unable according to the Grand Jury to "coherently explain."

We had before us a man named Goldberg, who conducted a store on Market Street, in Philadelphia. This man maintained an arsenal in his cellar . . . The evidence before us discloses that, on orders of Max Hoff, he supplied bulletproof vests and machine guns for which Hoff paid . . . We are advised Hoff cannot be prosecuted for his purchase of these weapons as no law makes their sale or possession unlawful.

After the repeal of Prohibition, Max Hoff, "often arrested but never jailed, often accused but never convicted," as the *New York Times* described him, was sued by the Internal Revenue Service for $33,000 in unpaid taxes. His home in Cobbs Creek Park was seized and sold for $1,500. His car was confiscated for a failure to pay $240 in garage rent. Arrested at the 30th Street Station for trying to pass a counterfeit twenty, and for flushing thousands more in bogus greenbacks down the toilet, he was found not guilty.

While the grand jury was sitting, Philadelphia's new mayor, Harry Arista Mackey, previously the head football coach at the University of Virginia and formerly a "wet," suddenly turned dry and ordered his police force to invade as many of the city's thirteen thousand speakeasies as they could over a single weekend. Grand jury or not, the results of the raid were the same as ever.

"Not only the mayor's feelings, but his spirits were considerably dampened," said the New York *Herald Tribune* after the swoop. "The sum total of the day's assaults was one man and one woman, captives in a raid on a disorderly house. Liquors of character were of course to be had."

* * *

"I want to serve notice now, in the presence of all concerned, that the murder of Hugh McLoon has by no means been dropped," Assistant District Attorney Thaddeus A. Daly declared in December, "after witness after witness who had been near the scene of the crime, including William Meister and Joseph Fries, refused to shed any light on the killing or its cause."

"Each of the killers will be tracked down, if it takes years," Daly thundered. "They will be punished, and so will all those who hold back information."

Except for the murdered O'Leary, they never would be. No one ever was convicted of the murder of Hughie McLoon.

Samuel Grossman's case was dismissed on September 12, the Commonwealth declaring it had been unable to link him to the murder.

"This man is not a gangster," Grossman's attorney fired back at the District Attorney. "This man is not a gunman. He is not a bootlegger. He is not a murderer. He is a respectable business man. He is the support of his widowed mother and five siblings. It has taken the Commonwealth a long time to admit they got the wrong man."

Jennie Brooks was sprung on September 28. "It is not too late for a reformation," Judge Lewis admonished the world-wise teen. She "fairly skipped along the aisle of the courtroom" as she departed.

Judge Lewis was overly optimistic. When history next heard from her, in May 1934, innocent ingénue Jennie Brooks was being arrested for trying to smuggle narcotics to her second (at least) husband, who was bunking at the House of Corrections in Holmesburg, Pennsylvania,

On October 2, 1928, Francis Peterson was sentenced to one year in prison in solitary confinement for carrying a concealed weapon. The charges of assaulting Detective Faries and Officer Wykoski were dropped.

"Why did you carry this loaded revolver?" Peterson was asked by a judge of the Quarter Sessions Court.

"In a resounding voice that could be heard in every part of the courtroom, Peterson replied, 'I carried it for protection. They had me tagged and were going to bump me off.'"

Ten days later, Shorty Feldman, pleading that his friends had deserted him and his parents were unable to afford his $7,500 bail, was released into the custody of his wife, Rose. They left the courtroom arm in arm, with Feldman promising to do right.

In December, four months after the deadly ambush in Jennie Brooks's bed, and ten weeks after the runaway bride was set free, the murder of Danny O'Leary was formally put to sleep. Detectives, it was reported, had been unable to find his slayer and key witness Jennie Brooks had disappeared.

* * *

Elizabeth Palmer McLoon Geatens, a sailor's daughter and a mother of three, outlived her first-born son by twenty-one years. She died at the age of sixty-three on October 1, 1949, of nutritional anemia and malnutrition caused by inoperable cancer of the stomach. She was placed with her Hughie at Holy Cross in Yeadon.

On August 1, 1957, Private Peter Geatens of the 3rd Infantry, a veteran of the Philippine Insurrection, fell (or was pushed) down the stairs at 1733 Johnston Street. He died three days later, aged seventy-two, at the U.S. Naval Hospital of "Traumatic Fracture—Skull."

Hughie's stepfather was buried at Holy Cross with his wife and her (if not his) idolized son. Dorothy would join them in the crowded grave in 1962.

Samuel Grossman, Doris Kearns's supposed boyfriend and the Callowhill Street garage owner who was suspected of driving the "big machine" from which Hughie McLoon was erased, was last heard from in 1932. He and his wife had been arrested for playing cards for money, but his wife argued in court that they had just come to the home where the game was in progress "to present her hostess with cheese dumplings."

On February 1, 1941, former Magistrate Edward P. Carney, later chief of the Division of Fines and Audits of the Philadelphia Department of Revenue, "ever ready with his tongue and his fists," was driving on the Pennsylvania Turnpike in Bedford County when his car rounded a curve and slammed into a parked vehicle owned by the Turnpike Commission. He was thrown from the car onto the shoulder of the road. He died at the scene of a fractured skull and broken neck. The Dancing Judge was fifty-three.

In April 1947, Benny Leonard was refereeing a full card of bouts at St. Nicholas Arena in the Borough of Queens, New York. He was fifty-one and already acclaimed as one of the greatest lightweight fighters in the sport's history, if one believes that boxing is indeed a sporting contest and not, as Bertrand Russell maintained, sadism in a satin robe. In the first round of the final match of the evening in the stifling, smoke-filled barn, Leonard suddenly crumpled to the ropes, then slid onto the canvas, grey-faced and motionless. "I'm afraid he's out for good," the ringside doctor whispered. Philosopher Russell, the pacifist, lived to ninety-seven and a half.

Connie Mack slowly passed in February 1956, two weeks short of his ninety-fourth birthday, three-quarters of a century after he had left East Brookfield, Massachusetts to try his hand at the still-new game of base ball. Through dynasties and desolation, fed by strategy and stinginess and sobriety and superstition, he endured as a monument to a simpler, slower America, and to a sport that needed no further perfection. Wrote Red Smith in the *Inquirer,* "There may never have been a more truly successful man."

Shorty Feldman engaged in a long and innovative criminal career, both organized and freelance. Weeks after being released in Hughie's death for lack of evidence, he was back in custody for a robbery at a Turkish bath, grabbing cash and jewelry while the customers were naked, and again, weeks later, for safecracking. Sent to Sing Sing in 1935 for grand larceny, Feldman later was caught stealing and forging blank prescription forms from a doctor's office to obtain narcotics. His attorney contended that the drugs were for Shorty's personal use and explained that his client "obviously is the subject of a great deal of inward stress."

He must have been. As soon as Feldman completed his sentence for the prescription-blank theft, he was transferred to federal authorities to begin serving a two-year stretch for his role in the heist of $1,800,000 in bonds from a Montreal bank.

Between pit stops in the pen, Feldman ran a (post-Repeal) saloon on Cuthbert Street called the Barbary Coast until its license was revoked in 1943, and he served as the business agent of Local 929 of the International Brotherhood of Teamsters: a role that saw him called as one of 1,526 witnesses to testify before the United States Senate's Select Committee on Improper Activities in Labor and Management. He died of lung cancer in 1960 at the age of fifty-two at the Philadelphia General Hospital.

"A guard was on duty in his room at all times."

EPILOGUE

"The Luckiest Boy In The World"

B ASEBALL'S AGE OF MAGIC did not end in 1918 when Hughie McLoon left Shibe Park for the Chester shipyard. On June 5 of the following year, at the Polo Grounds in Manhattan, a Brooklyn orphan named Eddie Bennett (who had lost both his parents to the Spanish Flu) was taking in a game from the bleachers when his grin amused the right fielder for the Chicago White Sox, Oscar Emil "Happy" Felsch. Eddie was a hunchback, and soon he would be a major-league mascot, perhaps the last of his stricken kind.

Like Rube Oldring with Louis Van Zelst, and Stuffy McInnis with Hughie McLoon, Felsch, who was turning twenty-eight, and Bennett, who was almost sixteen, bonded instantly. When the White Sox won the game 5–1, on an inside-the-park, grand-slam home run in the eighth inning by Eddie Collins (the same Captain Eddie of Connie Mack's $100,000 Infield), Happy Felsch rushed to notify the winning pitcher, Eddie Cicotte, that his new little deformed friend must have brought them luck.

The fact that, before the game started, the Yankees examined balls used by Cicotte "for foreign substances" also may have something to do with the outcome. Not that anyone ever would accuse the 1919 Chicago White Sox of cheating. Not in June, anyway.

Cicotte told Kid Gleason, the manager, about Eddie Bennett and, having no other attachments, his home and relations and source of sustenance a puzzle to all, the hunchback soon found himself on a train to Illinois as the full-time shaman of the South Side Sox. They won the American League pennant and then eight of them (give or take) conspired with New York gamblers to profane the national pastime and dump the holy World Series to the Cincinnati Reds. Among the Black Sox banished from the game forever were Cicotte and Felsch, along with Shoeless Joe Jackson, another of the Great War shipyard boys.

Bennett, it was reported, "suffered a blow to his prestige" when the heinous fix was revealed, but he sprang back quickly and, in 1920, transferred his incantations to his hometown Dodgers. They won the pennant, too.

But for miserliness in the face of prosperity, the Dodgers might have initiated a long string of championships right then. However, when the Brooklyns were too impecunious to ticket Eddie Bennett to Cleveland for the middle games of the World Series, and when they were beaten badly on the road, Bennett abdicated and cast a curse, as only hunchbacks could, on the team that would become known as Dem Bums. "They won't win again until I am dead," he uttered, or wished he had, and his prophecy came true.

In 1920, the Yankees acquired Babe Ruth. In 1921, they picked up free-agent batboy Eddie Bennett. From then on, with the two adolescents kneeling together in the on-deck circle and playing catch before every game, the Bronx Bombers were nearly unbeatable for a dozen years. Ruth transformed the sport with his extraterrestrial slugging, and he shook Eddie's hand each time he rounded third base on his ballerina legs and minced home.

The Yankees' ace Herb Pennock rubbed the mascot's hump for luck before each ascent of the pitcher's mound. "Smiling Eddie" ensured their karmic advantages, "mostly by crouching in front of the dugout and concentrating," according to a profile of the beaming young man in the *New Yorker* in 1932.

Like Louis and Hughie, Brownie and Clarence, Li'l Rastus and Sammy Kelly, and Lucky Williams before him, Bennett was "the envy of kids who wondered why Eddie got paid for what they considered a rare and wondrous privilege."

In 1923, Ruth deputized the mascot to carry a hand-written dinner invitation to an actress and model named Claire Hodgson, who was not the sort of broad he would be likely to encounter at Rose Hicks's sporting house in Philadelphia.

"You drink too much," Ms. Hodgson scolded the Babe on their first date.

"You sound like Miller Huggins," Ruth responded. They would be married for the rest of the Bambino's life.

Then, in the middle of the 1932 season, Eddie Bennett disappeared. Struck by a taxi on the Upper West Side of Manhattan, his legs and feet badly smashed, he was unable to crouch, play catch, or cast spells. He re-emerged on crutches in time for the World Series, but now, as a crippled cripple, his mascot days were done, and the Age of Magic ended with him.[34]

Eddie found consolation in alcohol, like millions before and since, Billy Sunday and his wife Ma be hanged.

By 1934, Eddie was drinking heavily and, still on the payroll of the Yankees to the sum of $100 per month, living in a first-floor apartment on West Eighty-Fourth Street.

"Why must you drink so much?" his landlady chastised him, a few days before Eddie Bennett was found dead in his bed in January

34 At the 2001 meeting of the American College of Sports Medicine in Baltimore, Dr. Edward McFarland of Johns Hopkins University reported that 44 percent of costumed sports mascots had "chronic back pain." It used to be that to become a mascot, a boy had to injure his spine. Now it is the Phanatic's turn to suffer.

1935. His room was a "darkened, cheerless" tomb "where a dim light cast a yellow glow on a wide picture of the triumphant Yankees of 1928." His walls "were covered with autographed pictures of ballplayers, scorecards, clippings of stories of games . . . and a drawer full of autographed baseballs, one of them signed by Babe Ruth."

"My feet hurt," the lucky hunchback had replied to his landlady.

* * *

In the spring of 1944, the New York Giants, John McGraw's old team, although he had been dead for a decade, brought in a young New Jersey athlete to tend the bats for the visiting clubs. Garth Garreau was a high school ballplayer and scholar, a budding chemical engineer, and not a hunchback. Time had leached the fantastic from the game, and the "lucky" children in their chronic pain.

When he graduated to the home team's clubhouse three years later, Garreau wrote a book called *Bat Boy of the Giants* that was so popular with the youth of America that it went through at least four printings.[35] This was his description of opening day:

> I felt like a dot in a horseshoe of faces. I was two eardrums in a world of roaring sound, and the sound nearly knocked me down . . . I saw an army of faces, faces, faces, all staring right at me and at nobody else.
>
> I took the bats across the field and I was like somebody in a daze. . .

Like the Mathewsons and Marquards who believed in Charlie Faust a generation earlier, Garreau's Giants were superstitious, too, but human deformity played no role in their jonahs and jinxes. A lucky

---

35 Garreau, Garth, *Bat Boy of the Giants* (New York, Comet Books, 1949).

undershirt, stepping on third base on the way to the outfield—these were the milder fetishes of the post-war, post-humpback game.

When his season as batboy of the Giants concluded, Garth went on to complete his engineering degree at Michigan State University and earned his wings as a United States Navy flier. In 1954, on a NATO training flight off the coast of Turkey, the wingtip of his aircraft caught the water, and the plane cartwheeled and exploded. All three members of the crew were killed. Only Garreau's body was recovered. Life is brief, and beautiful, and cruel, and baseball is its mirror.

On the final page of his awed and innocent bestseller from another time, the book that Little Van and Hughie McLoon and Eddie Bennett never got to write, Garth Garreau reproduced a telegram:

> I thought my bat boy story was finished but something wonder-ful has happened . . . I have just been told the Giants voted me a one-half share amounting to $171.40 STOP

I say again I'm the luckiest boy in the world.

* * *

Cuthbert is a forgotten little alley now, and the big metal door to number 927 is locked from the inside. The street is a campsite for the homeless, cold-shouldered by the back kitchens of Philadelphia's Chinatown. The corner where Hughie was shot in 1928 holds a parking garage, a construction site, the bus terminal, and a dreadful history that the city might prefer not to remember.

In the months and years that followed the murders of Hughie and Danny O'Leary, and the release of Messrs. Feldman, Peterson and Grossman for lack of evidence, numerous theories about the killing emerged.

There were hints from Assistant District Attorney Thaddeus Daly during the December 1928 coroner's inquest "that McLoon was killed because he refused to pay ten thousand dollars to some one that was not named."

"It had been reported," said the *Evening Bulletin,* "that O'Leary made a business of levying on saloons and speakeasies and actually holding up and robbing those that did not pay up.

"All those who were questioned on this point, however, denied knowledge."

In 1930, *True Crime Detective,* after devoting a disturbing number of column inches to Jennie Brooks's pink georgette outfit, concluded that the murder "arose from a quarrel between Grossman and his friends with McLoon over a girl for whom the garage owner had furnished a luxurious apartment in North Philadelphia." Both Grossman's garage and 1409 Jefferson Street are gone.

In 1937, Gordon Mackay, author of the "Is Zat So!" column in the Camden *Evening Courier,* claimed to have heard "the true story" from a police official.

McLoon, Mackay wrote, was "keen of wit, acid of tongue and bright as a button," but he signed his own death sentence when he "manhandled" Doris Kearns. The "beautiful girl," originally from Detroit, was the pet of Samuel Grossman, and so it was Grossman alone whose "snub-nosed gun peeked from the window," and whose "bullets bit into Hughie's broken body to snap the cord of life," no Danny, Shorty, or Francis necessary.

Mackay, unfortunately, dashed his own credibility by writing that Grossman later killed Mickey Duffy. That was a different Samuel Grossman.[36] Doris Kearns, Mackay added, died of tuberculosis.

---

36 In fact, there are at least seven separate men named Samuel Grossman in the Prohibition-era files at the Temple University library, including a Philadelphia poet who jumped out of a fifteenth-floor window because he wasn't making any money at his art.

In 1947, the syndicated columnist George Dixon recalled being assigned to cover McLoon's funeral. The "young hunchback," he wrote, "was walking down a side street with a couple of hot muggs when a car passed spurting machine gun lead. Hughie was riddled":

> My city desk had a tip that the killers might show up at the wake—this being another touching custom of gangdom. In fact it was quite cricket in those circles to knock off a guy providing you sent a wreath inscribed "We mourn our pal."

Suspicion fell on Duffy, the columnist claimed, to the extent that Dixon was ushered into a room by a couple of the beer baron's henchmen, handed a fifty-dollar bill, and commanded to write these words, verbatim: "Mickey Duffy contributed lavish."

"I pocketed the fifty," George Dixon affirmed. As Mark Twain wrote in *The Innocents Abroad*, "Virtue has never been as respectable as money."

In more recent times, McLoon has appeared here and there in works of crime fiction, such as *The Case of the Exploding Speakeasy* by David E. Fessenden, in which Hughie and Boo Boo Hoff assist Sherlock Holmes's brother Mycroft and Dr. Watson's son Thomas, a Philadelphia newspaperman, to "investigate the explosion and murders at the speakeasy, promising that when they learn who the culprit is, they'll 'take care of it.'"[37]

Today, in the new Roaring Twenties, the killing of Hughie McLoon remains a mystery, a tragedy best explained, perhaps, by a woman who never saw a ballgame. "I've often wondered," pleads hunchbacked Philip Wakem to the unattainable Maggie Tulliver in George Eliot's *The Mill on the Floss*, "whether you wouldn't really be

---

37 Fessenden, David E., *The Case of the Exploding Speakeasy* (Raleigh, Lighthouse Publishing of the Carolinas, 2013).

more likely to love a man that other women were not likely to love" a man who had been "marked from childhood for a peculiar kind of suffering, and to whom you were the day-star of his life."[38]

It may well be that Hughie McLoon's pursuit of another man's day-star—a mobster's easy moll—provoked the confrontation that led to the midnight ambush.

What we know for sure is that between two mortal falls, one from a playground seesaw, the other down the steps of Devine's Shoe Repair, a poor Irish kid from Leithgow Street won a gold watch and lost a father; strutted in moonlight, and died in the dark.

"The past alone is truly real," Bertrand Russell once said.

Funny, huh?

---

38 Eliot, George, *The Mill on the Floss* (New York, Penguin Classics, 2003).

ACKNOWLEDGEMENTS

Edward Morton is a lover of early twentieth-century Philadelphia baseball and, after a year of collaboration, a friend. His curiosity and passion for researching Hughie McLoon's brief life and tumultuous times made this book possible.

Parry Desmond has been writing about the shy and despicable "Boo Boo" Hoff for decades. Parry has been a generous and hospitable source of information on Prohibition and gangsterism in the Greene Country Towne.

Norman Macht spent more than a quarter-century absorbed in the life of Cornelius McGillicuddy. Norman's biographical trilogy of Connie Mack paints a true and tender portrait of baseball's patriarch.

Bob Schroeder, a colleague at the Canadian Broadcasting Corporation's current-affairs unit, has been fascinated by baseball's Age of Magic since he was a young fan in Cleveland. His fictionalized treatment *The Mascots of 1911: The Year God met the Devil in the World Series* was published in 2007.

Sincere thanks also to Arlene Balkansky and Erin Sidwell at the Library of Congress; Annie Anderson at the Eastern State Penitentiary Historic Site; Josue Hurtado at the Special Collections Research Center at the Temple University Libraries; to the many members of the Society for American Baseball Research whose carefully-researched biographies of the Mackmen of long ago form an essential part of this book; and to the Geatens and Klauder families of Pennsylvania and New Jersey, descendants of Hughie's half-brother Daniel and half-sister Dorothy.

Chris Ko welcomed a wanderer into Bob's Hardware at 2546 West Lehigh Avenue, four blocks from the shadow of Shibe Park, on the ground floor of the house where Hughie's grandma, Mary Munday McLoon, "surrounded by nearly two score of relatives" partied in 1912.

Oh, and if you notice the word "monsters" in this book, that was Lizzie's idea.

A NOTE ON SOURCES

Chapter One

The killing of McLoon and the retributive, forensic, and judicial developments that followed it were front-page news in Philadelphia for weeks. See, for a small sampling, the *Evening Bulletin*: "Hugh M'Loon Slain by Three Gunmen, 2 Companions Shot," August 9, 1928; "M'Loon Killing May Spark Gang War, Police Fear," Aug. 10; "M'Loon Funeral Monday," Aug. 11; "Hundreds Attend McLoon Funeral," Aug. 13; "5 Gunmen Kill Man Sought in M'Loon Murder," Aug. 15; "Motor Top Man Held As Suspect in M'Loon Murder," Aug. 16; "To Quiz Feldman in M'Loon Murder," Aug. 17; "6 Men, 2 Women Held Without Bail in Gang Murders," Aug. 18, with photos of the accused; "'Boo Boo' Hoff Called in Probe of Gang Murders," Aug. 19; "Wounded Gunman Tells in Hospital How McLoon Died – Says Gang Fights and Killings Are Always Over Liquor," Aug. 22;, and the *Bulletin* editorial, "The Gang Murder," Aug. 10.

See also "Hughie Hankered to Write," *Philadelphia Record*, Aug. 10; "McLoon Called Innocent Victim in Gang War," Aug. 11; "Thousands in Vigil on Hugh McLoon Dead in His Home," Aug. 14; "Bullet-Proof Car, Murder Squad at Hughie's Funeral," Aug. 14; "Refuses to 'Squeal' on M'Loon Slayer," Aug. 16; "3 Held in Gang Deaths as Judge Orders Probe Into Organized Crime," Aug. 17; "Five Charged With Murder of McLoon in Gang Warfare," Aug. 18.

See also "Notables Active on M'Loon Funeral," *Philadelphia Evening Public Ledger*, Aug. 10; "Police on Guard at M'Loon's Bier," Aug. 13; and "Scene of Splendor at M'Loon Viewing," *Philadelphia Inquirer*, Aug. 13.

For an introduction to Louis Van Zelst, Connie Mack, and baseball's Age of Magic, see "Crippled Boy is Athletics' Mascot," *Evening Bulletin*, Oct. 25, 1910; "Most Envied Boy in the Country," *Altoona Times,* Nov. 2, 1910; "Louis Van Zelst in the Age of Magic," John B. Holway, in *The National Pastime: A Review of Baseball History,* Volume 2, Society for American Baseball Research, 1983; "Connie Mack: Psychologist of Baseball," *New York Herald,* March 12, 1912; "The Stuff That Stars are Made of, by Connie Mack," *The Saturday Evening Post,* April 27, 1912; "Connie Mack's White Elephants and their Mascot," *Evening Bulletin,* March 21, 1915; Macht, Norman L., *Connie Mack and the Early Years of Baseball* (Lincoln, University of Nebraska Press, 2007) pp. 462-465.

Bertrand Russell's essay "On History" was published in the *Independent Review 3,* July 1904, pp. 207-15.

Wallace McCurley's interview with Hughie appeared in the *Evening Public Ledger* in the spring of 1922.

In addition to *The Strange Fate of Hughie McLoon: Famous Baseball Mascot* by Roger P. Butterfield, the July, 1930 issue of *True Detective Mysteries* included such stirring yarns as *The Great Chain Gang Escape, The Smashing of 'Little Egypt's' Gangster King,* and *Help Them Go Straight* by Franklin D. Roosevelt, Governor of New York.

Chapter Two

At the 1907 meeting of the New Year's Shooters and Councils' Special Committee, Hugh McLoon voted with the majority that "Despite the dissatisfaction of some of the clubs over the awards made last year, nearly all of the captains agreed that men would be preferable to women on the judges' stand on New Year's day."

Dr. Arthur Ames Bliss's *Blockley Days – Memories and Impressions of a Resident Physician,* was "Published for private circulation" in 1916.

"Largely poor" was the estimation of Lloyd M. Abernethy, associate professor of history, Beaver College (now Arcadia University) in his essay titled "Progressivism 1905-1919" in *Philadelphia: A 300-Year History* (New York, W. W. Norton and Co., 1982), page 527. "These new Philadelphians usually settled in the shabbiest sections," Prof. Abernethy noted.

Peter Geatens waited until 1934 to apply for an Army pension of $200 on the basis of his thirty-six-months' service in the 3rd U. S. Infantry, 1899-1902. He spelled his name as "Gatens" on the form.

For the history of the Bethel Burial Ground at Weccacoe Square, see Kristen De Groot, "Black Burial Site Discovered Under Philadelphia Playground to get Memorial," the Associated Press, July 5, 2018; National Register of Historic Places Registration Form, https://www.dot7.state.pa.us/CRGIS_Attachments/SiteResource/PA_Philadelphia_BethelBurialGround_nomination.pdf.

Chapter Three

The Old World provenance of America's National Pastime, long before its flowering in New York, New England, and Upper

Canada in the 1830s, is "proved" by Jane Austen's lament in 1803 in *Northanger Abbey* that her heroine Catherine Morland "should prefer cricket, base ball, riding on horseback . . . to books." Half a century before Austen, a British volume for children called *A Little Pretty Pocket-Book* already was comparing sluggers rounding third base and prancing "Home with Joy" to merchantmen who "for Lucre, fly over the Main; but with Pleasure transported, Return back again." But Puritan elders in Massachusetts were griping about kids playing "stoole ball and shuch-like sport" on Christmas Day on this side of the Atlantic as far back as the 1620s.

In 1846, in his earliest known writings on what he called "'base,' a certain game of ball," Whitman complained that "all classes seem to act as though there were no commendable objects of pursuit in the world except making money," and urged young men to spend an hour or two on the ballfield every day. But by 1889, he was inquiring of his amanuensis, Horace Traubel, "in base-ball, is it the rule that the fellow who pitches the ball aims to pitch it in such a way the batter cannot hit it? Gives it a twist—what not—so it slides off, or won't be struck fairly?" And on Tom's affirmative, Whitman said: "Eh? that's the modern rule then, is it? I should call it everything that is damnable."

Mack charged that McGraw's Baltimore Orioles "failed as a money maker through his own mismanaged and quarrelsome methods," and offered to bet him $1,000 that the A's would make a profit. There is no evidence that McGraw took the bet. Thirty-one years later, the two men managed against each other in the first All-Star Game.

"Parade In Athletics' Honor One Of The Greatest Tributes Ever Paid By Philadelphia," hollered the *Inquirer* of the grand defile. "It was a great night for Connie Mack and his victorious team," the broadsheet gushed. "It was a great night for The Inquirer, the people's paper and the advocate of clean, honest ball," it crowed. The *Inquirer,* of course, sponsored the parade. "Cold type fails to do it justice," the journal sighed.

Chapter Four

In 2009, the U.S. National Library of Medicine of the National Institutes of Health published an *Historical Overview of Spinal Deformities in Ancient Greece* that details the diagnoses and treatments that are attributed to Hippocrates. See https://www.ncbi.nlm. nih.gov/pmc/articles/PMC2654856/

For the saga of little Leon Abeomontz, see *Philadelphia Inquirer,* June 16, 1901.

Rabelais also calls Triboulet "Hair-brained, Talmudical, Algebraical, Well-Hung and Timbered, Arctic, Pimpled, Freckled," and about a hundred other things. See: https://www.gutenberg.org/ files/1200/1200-h/1200-h.htm#link32HCH0038

See *Velázquez, Dwarves, and the Contradiction of Graceful Painting* by Daniel A. Siedell, posted on September 4, 2012 to pantheos. com: https://www.patheos.com/blogs/cultivare/2012/09/velasquez-dwarfs-and-the-contradiction-of-graceful-painting/

For Lavinia Warren's disdain of being petted, see Kim E. Nielsen, *A Disability History of the United States* (Beacon Press, 2012), page 90. See also Susan Schweik, *The Ugly Laws: Disability in Public* (New York, New York University Press, 2009).

In the Charleston incident, as reported in the *Philadelphia Inquirer* of June 13, 1913, sixteen-year-old hunchback Frank Carter challenged his tormentor, a boy named Miller, to a duel with sharpened pokers. Miller "received a thrust through the heart" and died. Carter, seriously wounded, managed to flee, after other boys "apologized to him for their actions of the past."

According to the *Harrisburg Patriot* of November 19, 1910, twelve-year-old Michael Rolemius was "mistaken for a dog in the gathering dusk last evening" and was "run over by a heavy delivery wagon after having been knocked down by the horses of a wagon just preceding. Death was instantaneous."

The Monte Cross crossed-bats anecdote of 1900 appeared in *Sporting Life*, quoting the *Saint Louis Star*.

James Hart of the Louisville Colonels told the story of the jonah who picked up the bats too soon to a reporter from the *San Francisco Chronicle* during a winter barnstorming trip in 1886. Thom Karmik's blog, BaseballHistoryDaily.com, is the delightful source of this and dozens of other tales of superstition, ritual, and diamond folklore. The site is a truly valuable lode of what Karmik calls "the forgotten history of the national pastime."

"The carrying of mascots by the various clubs has gone out of fashion somewhat," the *Chicago Post* added in 1889. "It originated in the wild and woolly West, and for the next two years afterwards every first class club had a mascot. The style ran to freaks of nature, and a dwarf, a humpback, or a giant was sure of an engagement and a good salary. As the game advances each year the class of ball players are improving and are men of better education than formerly, and are losing a great many of the particularities which formerly distinguished them."

According to the *Washington Post*, Big Bill Lange secured his magic poult "out of a crop of 13 eggs set to hatch in the dark of the moon."

The bird, however, was reported dead when Lange arrived at Spring Training in March, 1896. The despondent outfielder's batting average dropped sixty points to .326 and his Colts clucked their way to a dismal fifth-place finish.

See also: "Major League Baseball Players are Superstitious," *Bellingham Herald,* September 5, 1919; "Base Ball Superstitions," *Philadelphia Times,* September 19, 1886; "The Things That Bring Luck to the Various Clubs," *Saint Louis Post-Dispatch,* 1886, quoted in www.baseballhistorydaily; "Are Base Ball Players Superstitious?" *Harrisburg Telegraph,* 1884, quoted in www.baseballhistorydaily; "Mascots and Hoodoos Strange Superstitions Prevalent Among Sporting Men," *Idaho Statesman,* November 16, 1893; "Ball Players Superstitions Many Charms Resorted To," *Bismarck Daily Tribune,* May 18, 1889; "Odd Mascots in Major Leagues; Boys, Birds, Dogs and Geese Popular," Hugh B. Fullerton, *Wilkes-Barre Times Leader,* May 8, 1914; "Baseball Mascots in the Nineteenth Century," Larry G. Bowman, in *The National Pastime: A Review of Baseball History,* Society for American Baseball Research, Volume 19, 1999, page 108

When the stalwarts flexed their lumps of muscle in Egypt, the players had to battle local spectators for possession of their only baseball each time it was fouled into the crowd. "I apologized to the Sphinx on behalf of my team," said losing manager Cap Anson. "To this she turned a deaf ear."

For the *Topeka State Journal* quotation, more on Willie Hahn and Willie Hume, and the profusion of black mascots with Ontario teams in the 1880s, see Chris Bateman, "Historicist: Toronto's First Baseball Mascot," May 14, 2016: https://torontoist.com/2016/05/historicist-the-first-toronto-baseball-mascot/

For more on Brownie Burke, see the excellent SABR biography by Phil Williams: https://sabr.org/bioproj/person/317716b0

"Base-ball, the one life-passion of little Sammy Kelly, was the cause of his death," lamented the *Philadelphia North American* on August 13, 1903.

"It is a better plan to aim to prevent these deformities than to seek means of supporting the unfit," reasoned Dr. Krusen in his introduction to *Short Talks on Personal and Community Health*, F. A. Davis Co., Philadelphia,1920. See also: "Advocates Advice to Young Parents; Health Director Asserts Many Defects in Children Can Thus Be Avoided," *Philadelphia Inquirer,* November 13, 1916.

Chapter Five

In his article "The Girl Army: The Philadelphia Shirtwaist Strike of 1909-1910," Daniel Sidorick of Temple University quotes a letter to the *Public Ledger* by a Bryn Mawr woman named Louise Elder: "No lover of stirring and inspiring sights should lose a mass-meeting of the Philadelphia shirt-waist strikers. To sit where one faces these young people, tier upon tier, as they listen, absorbed and unself-conscious, to the speakers – how strange and new and shining in this corrupted and weary city." (*Pennsylvania History*, vol. 71, No. 3, July 2004) See https://sites.temple.edu/womenushist/2016/02/15/the-girl-army-the-philadelphia-shirtwaist-strike-of-1909-1910-by-daniel-sidorick/

The corner of Broad and Spring Garden, scene of "a clash between the mob and police" in 1910, is the same intersection where so many serpentines were flung in celebration of the A's pennant in 1902 that horses were hobbled and tripped.

See *The New York Times*, February 20, 1910: "Mob rule prevailed throughout the city to-day. A score of riots in which the police and strikers resorted even to shooting sent nearly a hundred persons to hospitals."

To Cobb's biographer, Al Stump, the Georgia Peach was "thoroughly maladjusted." Writing of Cobb in 1995, Paul Hemphill said that his demeanor, "both on the field and off . . . would have given even an Adolf Hitler pause . . . Paranoid, racist, belligerent, mean beyond our wildest nightmares, he delivered thrashings to umpires, opposing players, teammates, fans, his wives and children, clubhouse attendants, policemen, bartenders, cab drivers, hotel desk clerks, even dogs and horses. It is quite likely that he killed at least one man." In *My 66 Years in the Big Leagues* (Philadelphia, Universal House, 1950), Connie Mack called Cobb "the greatest who ever lived . . . a fiery and fearless player." In 1928, after leaving Detroit under the cloud of a game-fixing scandal, Cobb would finish his career at age forty-two as Mack's right fielder, but he would serve only as an occasional pinch-hitter in August and September of that final campaign. The Peach went out batting .323, his lowest average since 1906.

"I've walked along the street with ball-players and seen them stop a young negro and take off his hat and run their hands through his kinky hair," Mathewson wrote in *Pitching in a Pinch, Or Baseball From the Inside* (New York, Grosset and Dunlap, 1912). "Then I've seen the same ball-player go out and get two or three hits that afternoon and play the game of his life. Again, it is the confidence inspired, coupled with the ability."

For more on Louis Van Zelst, see the notes for Chapter One, above.

See "Gives Luck Charm to Athletics; Without It Goes to Tragic Death" by Si Sanborn, *Chicago Tribune,* December 28, 1910. "Doesn't that set one thinking a bit?" Sanborn quotes American League president Ban Johnson. Chief Horan's widow Margaret outlived him by forty-seven years.

Chapter Six

Christy Mathewson unpacks (and embellishes) the Faustian legend in *Pitching in a Pinch*. See also: "C. Victory Faust Makes His Debut with Giants," *New York Herald*, October 8, 1911; "Quaker Fans Outdo Giant Followers In Outbursts of Joy," *New York Evening World*, October 16, 1911; "Big Chief's Single Stirs Dull Crowd out of Drab Spirit," *New York Evening World*, October 17, 1911; Schecter, Gabriel, *Victory Faust: The Rube Who Saved McGraw's Giants* (Charles April Publications, 2006) and Schecter's SABR article about Faust, https://sabr.org/bioproj/person/d1ee8535

For the 1911 World Series and the existential clash between Faust and Louis Van Zelst, see "Wonderful Fans: Hunchback For A Mascot," by the 10th Marquis of Queensberry, *Washington Star*, October 15, 1911; "World's Series Is On," *Brooklyn Daily* Eagle, October 14, 1911; "Mascots Meet," *York Gazette*, October 18, 1911; "As the 37,000 Saw the Game," *New York Sun*, October 18, 1911; "Athletics Uphill Victory," *New York Sun*, October 25, 1911. For an engaging comparison of the lives and careers of Mack and McGraw, see "Incarnations of Success" in Tygiel, Jules, *Past Time: Baseball as History* (New York, Oxford University Press, 2000), pages 35-63.

Queensberry was especially enamored of the females in the throng. "They must have come from Philadelphia," he wrote of one pair. "They have such good lungs."

For Marquard's allegation that Little Van was stealing Giants catcher Chief Meyers's signs, see "Notes and Gossip of World's Series Games," *Wilkes-Barre Record*, October 23, 1911.

For Home Run Baker's bat and Little Van's share of the World Series prize money, see Strawbridge & Clothier advertisement, *Philadelphia Inquirer*, November 1, 1911, page 7; "Athletics Reward

Young Mascot," *Wilkes-Barre Times Leader,* October 28, 1911; and "Scribblings From Bub's Scorecard," October 31, 1911 in the same.

For Mr. Ralph Waldo Emerson Johnnie Baked Beans Connor, see "Field Secretary of Boston Braves," *Chicago Tribune,* October 14, 1914; "Mascot Is A 'Highbrow' – Youngster Uses Spectacles and the Broad A," *Baltimore Evening Sun,* October 8, 1914; "Braves Share Their Riches – Remember All, Down to the Bat Boy," *Boston Globe,* October 17, 1914.

For the Death of Louis Van Zelst, see "Little Louie Van Zelst, Late Mascot of Athletics, Was Real Pal of Players," *Pittsburgh Daily Post,* March 23, 1915; "Death Ends Suffering of Noted Mascot," "Floral Tokens at Bier of Athletic Mascot," "Athletics Disconsolate Over Louie's Death," and "Mack's Grief Great at Mascot's Death," *Philadelphia Press,* March 21, 1915; "Mack's Little Mascot Dies," *Philadelphia Bulletin,* March 21, 1915.

"The Mackmen plan to keep the memory of Little Louis Van Zelst green and fragrant," reported the *Evening Public Ledger.*

For Raoul Naughton, see "Raoul, the Real Rooter, is Mascot of the Phillies," *Philadelphia Evening Public Ledger,* October 7, 1915 and Berton Braley's poem entitled "Raoul Naughton Official Chaser of Philly Jinx – Hunchbacked Mascot of Moran's Men No Longer Unhonored and Unsung" in the same newspaper on October 9, 1915, to wit:

> *You won't find Raoul Naughton on the scorecard any place,*
> *He's never sent a homer soaring into space.*
> *He never scooped a grounder and he never caught a fly,*
> *As it hurtled swiftly earthward from the clear and azure sky.*

And so on for another fifty-four verses.

Chapter Seven

The *Registrum Matrominium* at Our Lady of the Sacred Heart shows that Petrum Geatens and the widow Elizabeth McLoon were married in the church on January 19, *consensu habito per verba di praesente,* one day before their civic registration.

For Billy Sunday's sidewalk conversion to abstinence, see Okrent, Daniel *Last Call – The Rise and Fall of Prohibition* (New York, Scribner, 2010), pp.96-97. Connie Mack was born one month after Billy Sunday and outlived him by a quarter-century.

For Sunday's 1915 crusade in his Philadelphia tabernacle and his visit to the city's leading families, see "'Come On, Lobsters,' Challenges Sunday; 60,000 Chant Amens," *Philadelphia Evening Public Ledger,* January 4, 1915; "'Church Vote Keeps Saloon From Hell,' Sunday Thunders," Jan. 5; "Student Host in University Gymnasium Listens to 'Billy' Sunday Roast College Sins," Jan. 8; "Sunday Hurls Shafts of Fire at Sin's Shame," Jan. 14; "Sunday Assails Priests of Gold Who Mock God," Jan. 15; "Sunday Scores Big Hit With Society Folk," Jan. 21.

While the Drexel Biddles were entertaining the apostle of abstemiousness, automation was putting droves of less well-heeled Americans out of work. See "More than 200 of city's homeless men sleeping on floor in factory," *Philadelphia Evening Public Ledger,* January 4, 1915. For Sunday's reaction, see "Sunday Hits at Shams in Pleading for Living Wage," *Philadelphia Evening Public Ledger,* Jan. 23. Of the floor-sleepers' sisters, Sunday declared, "I don't believe there are many girls who are working for six dollars a week, a dollar a day, wearing the clothes they are wearing, paying the room rent they are paying, and doing it all on the small salary . . . If they are driven to make a little money on the side to exist, who's to blame them? Who has driven them to do it?"

For an academic analysis of the relationship between the baseball and brewing industries, see Saethre, Steinar, *Baseball and Beer: An Independent Study*, SUNY Cortland, 2008.

Baseball-Reference.com calls Charlie Sweeney "a rock star before his time." Sweeney's manager at Providence in 1884, Frank Bancroft, told the *Boston Post* decades later about the game in which a drunken Sweeney refused to leave the mound. See https://baseballhistorydaily. com/2014/08/22/in-their-own-words-frank-bancroft/

Delahanty's obit and the details of his maritime dismemberment, originally published in *The New York Times* on July 10, 1903, can be found at https://www.baseball-almanac.com/deaths/ed_delahanty_ obituary.shtml

For the ballfield, theater, and pleasure-house career of Lew "The Hoss" Brown, see Bob LeMoine's SABR biography https://sabr.org/ bioproj/person/457fa2e8

"When my mother realized that my heart was so set, she reluctantly consented with secret misgivings," Mack writes in *My 66 Years in the Big Leagues*. "'Promise me one thing,' she said. 'Promise me that you won't drink.' That promise I will keep to the end of my life."

For a selection of Mack's own writings on abstinence, see *The Temperance Cause*, June 1914; "The Secret of Success in Baseball," *Scientific Temperance Journal*, 1912, page 116. See also "The Life of a Ballplayer," by Eddie Collins in *The National Sunday Magazine*, 1914. For Collins's "Ten Rules of Life," see https://baseballhistorydaily. com/2015/10/05/collins-ten-commandments/ "Life is a whole lot like playing baseball under Connie Mack's orders," Collins said in Palmyra, N.J.

For Wilson's Convention Hall speech, see "President Wilson's Peace Chant," *Philadelphia Evening Public Ledger*, May 11, 1915;

"President Gives Message of Peace to Nation; Kaiser Charged with Murder by Coroner's Jury," and "Wilson Declares Nation Can Be Too Proud to Fight," *Philadelphia Inquirer*, May 11, 1915.

For the suit alleging damage to Billy Sunday's rented house, see "Things Declared Gone Range From 26 Whisky Glasses to a Marble Dog," *Philadelphia Evening Public Ledger*, May 11, 1915; See also "'Damnable lie,' Says Ma – 'I'll Punch Your Face,'" *Washington Herald*, May 12, 1915.

Chapter Eight

According to Bruce Kuklick in *To Every Thing A Season*, "Shibe not only wanted a product strong enough to withstand the yearly weight of hundreds of thousands of fans . . . it was 'a lasting monument' built to endure, with a grandiose beauty that should express continuing prosperity and assured advance." (Page 25) Shibe Park was renamed Connie Mack Stadium in 1953 and served as home field for the A's until 1954, when they moved to Kansas City, and for the Phillies from 1938 to 1970. The 'lasting monument' was torn down in 1976. The site now is occupied by the Deliverance Evangelistic Church.

The few snippets of McLoon's speech that were rendered into typeface in his lifetime had him yipping in a scampish argot unencumbered by the 'th' in such words as 'that' and 'them.' By comparison, the holy Louis Van Zelst never was quoted downgrading "you" into "yuh" or "used to" into "us'ta."

The A's victory on the day of Hughie's debut coincided with the arrival in Baltimore of the German merchant submarine *Deutschland*, which had traveled all but ninety miles of its journey from Heligoland under water. "Jules Verne was right after all," joshed Robert W.

Maxwell in the *Evening Public Ledger.* "Yesterday afternoon when the down-trodden, much-maligned, collegiate ball club representing our city trimmed, defeated, torpedoed, sunk, walloped and beat another ball club representing Saint Louis . . . Anything can happen these days and those two historic events prove it."

The steep, sudden fall from first place of such champions as McInnis and Mack would be metrically kidded, but not cruelly mocked, by wordsmiths Rice, Lardner, Runyan, et al. "The age of cynicism had not dawned," writes Norman Macht in *Connie Mack: The Turbulent and Triumphant Years.*

"Connie Mack was great in victory and he is great in defeat," said the *New York Evening Journal* as the Athletics went eight and twenty-three in August, 1916. "We admire him for it." In the *New York Globe,* a cartoon by Robert Ripley, three years before he inaugurated his *Believe It Or* Not feature, predicted the Mackmen going from "some scream" in 1916 to "some team" in 1917.

"The rookies were not allowed in the clubhouse," Macht notes. The new mascot, of course, would have been an exception.

If you think you can endure a day-by-day accounting of the Athletics' 1916 season, replete with Weart's sad dispatches to *The Sporting News,* see John G. Robertson, *A's Bad As It Gets: Connie Mack's Pathetic Athletics of 1916* (McFarland, 2014)

"Jim Nasium" was the pen name of Edgar Forrest Wolfe, a cartoonist who was trained at the Pennsylvania Academy of Fine Arts.

It was at 2546 West Lehigh that in November, 1912, "desiring to gather around her at least once more her many nephews, nieces and grandchildren, Mrs. Mary McLoon, the aged aunt of Hugh McLoon, attache of Quarter Sessions Court, gave a house party last Sunday evening. Mrs. McLoon, although nearly eighty years old, entered into the festivities of the evening and proved a gracious host. She was surrounded by nearly two score of relatives," *Philadelphia Inquirer*, November 10, 1912. Grandson Hughie would have been ten and a half. The row house still stood in 2020, with Bob's Hardware occupying the ground floor and the two upper levels boarded-up and vacant.

Chapter Nine

The "particularly bad grace" letter was signed "A Fan Who Reads 'Em All," published on September 15, 1916. The A's had a record of 30-107 the day it ran.

Wallace McCurley's interview of McLoon for the *Evening Public Ledger* in 1922 is the prime surviving evidence of Hughie's repartee.

For the polio outbreak of 1916, see "Plague Cases Here Mount to More Than 100," *Evening Public Ledger*, August 8, 1916. See also "Five More Die of Baby Plague," *Evening Public Ledger*, Aug. 29.

Had just 1,887 California voters chosen Hughes over Wilson, the bearded iceberg would have been elected. Of course, had the A's won only fifty-five more ballgames, they would have captured the 1916 pennant.

At Washington Square, the principal speaker on the theme of "Liberty At Any Cost" was Rev. John J. Wheeler, new rector of the Church of Our Lady of Mount Carmel.

The *Inquirer's* report on "Kiss the Flag!" appeared on April 4, 1917. The *Evening Public Ledger's* report of the same incident had "women members" of the Red Cross urging men to enlist when "an unidentified German" insults the Stars and Stripes. The crowd "growled with rage," the *Ledger* reported.

For the Eddystone tragedy, see "119 Killed, 150 Injured, Majority Women, By Explosion Laid to Plotters in Plant," and "Martial Law Now for Philadelphia, Eddystone Explosion Brings Drastic Wartime Measures Here," *Philadelphia Inquirer*, April 11, 1917.

See "Shibe Park Non-Ad Rule Broken For Navy's Call," *Evening Public Ledger*, May 30, 1917, page 12.

For anti-German episodes and war hysteria, see "Finnish Laborers at Bristol Admitted Sympathies Were With the Kaiser," *Philadelphia Inquirer*, April 26, 1917. "Strenuous Treatment for Bond Slackers; One Hanged to Tree," April 29; "Tarred, Feathered, and Charged With Sedition," and "Their Teutonic Ardor Chilled By Fire Hose," May 1. See also "Her Children Teased, Woman Seeks Death," *Evening Public Ledger*, September 29, 1917.

For the racial killings, see "Three More Shot in Chester Riots, Guards in Control," *Philadelphia Press,* July 28, 1917, "2 Slain, 20 Injured as 5000 Fight Race Riot in South Phila," *Philadelphia Inquirer,* July 29; and "Fourth Man Dies Victim of Race Riots Downtown" and "Sailors Beat Negroes, Causing Excitement in Shadow of City Hall," in the Aug. 1 and Aug. 9 editions of the same paper.

F. C. Lane noted that "Our Civil War made baseball America's national sport. The soldiers played baseball in their leisure hours and when they disbanded, they carried home with them a lasting love for the game." An accompanying photograph in *Baseball Magazine* showed Doughboys posing at home plate in gas masks. See https://baseballhistorydaily.com/2019/08/16/baseball-thrives-on-war/

Stuffy McInnis hit 20 home runs in 19 major-league seasons. Sammy Sosa of the Cubs juiced 20 homers in the month of June, 1998, alone.

Chapter Ten

Contrary to the *Inquirer's* report of an exploding boiler, the *Reading News-Times* noted on April 20, 1918 that McLoon was "severely burned while heating some water" when he "placed a pan on an oil stove and, as he applied a match, the stove exploded." Hughie "was removed to the Women's Homeopathic Hospital. He will recover."

"The duties of a manager or a player are nothing compared with the burden carried by that very important part of the machine – the mascot," the *Ledger* joshed.

Re: "Collected a game" In August, 1916, when Connie's woebegone kindergarteners finally did win one, the *New York Journal* delighted:

> *Stranger than tales of piratical bands cruising the Spanish Main*
> *Stranger than stories of bad Western lands where good men die young or are slain*
> *Stranger than word from explorers heard or soldiers of fortune and fame*
> *Is this little story—say, Bo, it's a bird - The Macks have collected a game!*

For the entire poem, see https://www.thegoodphight.com/2017/6/2/15721502/philadelphia-phillies-2017-athletics-1916-terrible

Like Peter Geatens, Crowder was a veteran of the Philippine Insurrection, serving as a judge advocate. In 1916, Baker told the Reserve Officers Association that "I am a pacifist. I am a pacifist in my hope; I am a pacifist in my prayers; I am a pacifist in my belief that God made man for better things than that a civilization should always be under the blight of this increasingly deadly destruction which war leaves us." See the Smithsonian Institution's blog: https://

americanhistory.si.edu/blog/capsules-world-war-i and http://www.thisgreatgame.com/1918-baseball-history.html

For baseball and the military draft, see "The Old Sport's Musings," *Philadelphia Inquirer*, April 29, 1918; "Players Should Join the Army," *Inquirer*, May 7, 1918; "Waiters, Servants, Bartenders, Store Clerks, Race Track Followers and Possibly Baseball Players Among Those Affected By Regulation," *Inquirer*, May 24, 1918. Jim Nasium's cartoon of May 24 showed a nervous, nail-chewing ballplayer being offered a choice between "the old firearm" and "the old dinner pail" by Provost Marshall Gen. Crowder. See also "Barry's Team Disbands," *Inquirer*, April 24, 1918.

On August 6, 1918, the hottest day ever recorded in Philadelphia at 103.2 degrees, agents of the Department of Justice searched the Shibe Park grandstand for slackers during a boxing match. See "1200 Men Arrested in Ball Park Raid on Draft Dodgers," *Philadelphia Inquirer*, August 7, 1918. Two days later, the mercury reached 106.2. Twenty-five thousand shipbuilders walked off the job at Hog Island. See also "Hog Islanditis," *New York Tribune*, October 7, 1918.

For the Bethlehem Steel and Delaware River Shipbuilding leagues as refuges for major-league stars, see the authoritative SABR articles by Brian McKenna and Jim Leeke, respectively: https://sabr.org/bioproj/topic/bethlehem-steel-league and https://sabr.org/research/delaware-river-shipbuilding-league-1918. "Jackson, especially, became a lightning rod for condemnation," Leeke observed.

One of the first former A's to enlist was Jack Nabors, a hard-luck hurler from Alabama who lost nineteen consecutive decisions for the 1916 Athletics. "I am glad to have the chance to do my bit with the rest of the red-blooded Americans," Nabors said. He spent the summer at a training camp in Iowa. In the winter, he contracted the Spanish Flu. His lungs never healed. He died of tuberculosis in 1923.

For the impeachment of Kris Kringle, See "Progressivism 1905-1919," in *Philadelphia: A 300-Year History*, page 560.

It has been accepted for more than a century that Mathewson survived the gas-mask drill and the war but that tuberculosis invaded his ravaged lungs and he never fully regained his health. In and out of baseball as a Giants coach and principal owner of the Boston Braves, he moved to Saranac Lake, N.Y. for treatment at the Trudeau Sanitorium and died there on the first day of the 1925 World Series. For recent scholarship casting doubt that Mathewson was harmed by gas in France, see https://www.insidesources.com/did-baseball-great-christy-mathewson-die-of-chemical-warfare/

Too splenetic to succumb to mere poison, Cobb lived until 1961.

Phil Williams profiled the peripatetic Rope Perry for SABR: https://sabr.org/bioproj/person/55c35b63

Moriarty's most famous inspirational poem, still posted in many locker rooms, was entitled *The Road Ahead or the Road Behind*: "It's you and I who make our fates, we open up or close the gates. . ."

In the *Evening Public Ledger* of September 5, 1918, Hughie advertised for baseball teams of twelve and thirteen-year-olds to play his "Chester-Heater Boys of the Chester Shipbuilding Company." It is the first available evidence of his freelance mascotting and team-management career. He had just turned sixteen.

For the Spanish Flu in Philadelphia, see "Spanish Influenza Sends 600 Sailors to Hospital Here," *Philadelphia Inquirer*, September 19, 1918, "Fourteen New Victims of Influenza at Dix," Sept. 23; "Spanish Influenza Is Fatal to 26 Dix Men," Sept. 25; "Day's Influenza Death Toll 289," Oct. 7; "Siege of Influenza at Breaking Point," Oct. 16; "Churches Reopen Sunday and Schools Monday," Oct. 25; "Grip Killed 711 in One Day," Oct. 28; "City Departments

Unite to Thwart Undue Enthusiasm When Saloons Reopen," Oct. 29; "Influenza Epidemic Grows Rapidly Worse" and "Influenza Isolated at Chester Shipyard," *Evening Public Ledger,* Oct. 1; "Director Krusen Takes Radical Step to Combat Disease," Oct. 3; "Saloons Shut at 7 Tonight By Grip Order" and "Telephone Service Faces a Crisis," Oct. 4.

Dr. Wilmer Krusen wouldn't die of anything until 1943.

Chapter Eleven

For the dueling hunchbacked mascots of Los Angeles fisticuffs, see "Rivers Knocks Out Brown in 10th of Vicious Fight," *New York Herald,* February 23, 1913, page 18.

The *Reading News-Times* of October 8, 1920, reported that "Chuck Jannetti has taken Hughey McLoon in tow as mascot. Hughey used to be the Athletics bat boy." A few weeks later, the teen made the rounds of the Philly papers, bringing the news that "Tommy Loughlin (*sic*) of St. Monica's C.C. is booked to box at the National New Year's Day, according to Hughey McLoon." See also, "Loughran Hopes to Fight Dempsey," *Evening Bulletin,* August 4, 1928 (five days before Hughie's murder). For Jannetti's violent death, see "Fatally Wounded While Attempting to Knock Gun out of Hand of Bandit," *Hazelton Plain Speaker*, February 16, 1931, page 9.

The *Evening Public Ledger* of May 18, 1921 reported on the McLoon-Dempsey negotiations. The mayor of Atlantic City is quoted as saying that Hughie "probably will get the job." He didn't. King, a "heavyweight bulldog," was identified in the Ogden (Utah) *Evening Standard* as "a gift from a Toledo admirer." See http://americasdog. blogspot.com/2012/02/jack-dempsey.html?m=1

For the 1920 Olympic anecdote, see "Treatment of Athletes in Antwerp Was Terrible, Says Philadelphia Boxer," *Evening Public Ledger*, September 20, 1920, page 18. Hughie is called "McGloon" and is mentioned only once, possibly as an inside joke. There is no firm evidence that he ever left American *terra firma* in his life.

Benny Leonard's bare-knuckle typewriter battle with Bertrand Russell began with Russell's interview by Edna B. Mann in the *New York World* of January 8, 1928. "Doesn't the world need this delight?" Ms. Mann asked the philosopher, striking a nerve. See "Benny Leonard Disagrees With Bertrand Russell on Boxing, *Literary Digest*, 96, No. 11, March 17, 1928, pages 58-60. See also Franklin Foer, "Mama Said Knock You Out" in *Jewish Jocks: An Unorthodox Hall of Fame* (New York. Twelve, Hachette Book Group, 2012) and *Boxing: Medical Aspects,* edited by Friedrich Unterharnscheidt and Julia Taylor Unterharnscheidt (Academic Press, April, 2003)

For the McLoon-Leonard-Tendler love triangle, see "Hughey McLoon Will be Leonard's Mascot," *Camden Morning Post*, July 28, 1921. McLoon's bylined essay appeared in, among other papers, the Bridgewater (New Jersey) *Courier-News* of August 8, 1921: "Benny's Mascot is Confident."

Carney first was elected to the magistracy as a "minority party candidate;" i.e., not a Republican, in 1919 at the age of 31. A newspaper report said that he had been orphaned at the age of eight "and he obtained work as a messenger boy" before being hired as a courier at City Hall, where he spent the rest of his life.

For the olive oil incident, see "Midget Mascot Aids Poth's Team," *Evening Bulletin*, November 8, 1919. Another of Hughie's putative substitute father-figures, Frank Poth, partial heir to the Poth Brewing Company fortune, automobile racer, *bon vivant*, and skirt-chaser extraordinaire, spent much of the first three decades of the twentieth century suing and being sued by partners and debtors he had stiffed, by the federal government for tax evasion, and by his own brothers.

For examples of McLoon's athletic endeavors, see "Braves and Scouts Both Win Fast Games," and "Double Triumph for Parkside Reserves," in *Camden Courier*, November 10, 1920 and December 6, 1920 respectively.

The "tiniest manager" title was awarded by the *Inquirer* on August 2, 1925, page 6. See also James Isaminger's "Ringside Close-Ups" in the *Inquirer* of August 11, 1925, page 13. For Hughie's promotion of Alex Hart as a "clever fistman," see "Manager Declares Danny is Not Afraid of Philadelphia," *Camden Evening Courier*, August 8, 1925 and "Camden Attracts Pugilistic Stars," in the same newspaper August 18.

For the "ballot crooks," see the *Inquirer* of October 7, 1925, page 16. On December 11, a photograph in the *Inquirer* showed McLoon, in a sharp-lapelled, double-breasted suit, holding a hat from which members of the "newly-elected minor judiciary" draw lots for their court assignments. Edward P. Carney had his hand in the derby as the picture was snapped.

For the sportswriters' billiard tournament, see *Philadelphia Inquirer*, February 14, 1924, page 18. For "the wing-footed mercury," see the *Inquirer* of Feb. 29 page 23. "A handier man cannot be found around these diggings," the paper said of Hughie McLoon.

Chapter Twelve

For the flapper raid, see the front page of the *Philadelphia Inquirer*, March 1, 1926. Thirty-four young party-goers were arrested. "All gave fictitious names," the paper noted.

For Billy Sunday's premature exultation, see Okrent, page 117. Lane's lament is quoted on page 3, *ibid*. Denied the succor of a warming flask, it took only fifteen months for Prohibition, and heart disease, to claim the Secretary in the spring of 1921 at the age of 56.

Exposing Philadelphia as the nation's most egregious exemplar of 100-proof corruption furnished employment to dozens of writers and moralists from across the country, long after Lincoln Steffens left town. For example, see "Phila. Is Worst Vice City, Police to Blame," *Philadelphia Inquirer*, April 1, 1918; "How Wet is Pennsylvania?" *Literary Digest* No. 79, November 10, 1923; "Why They Cleaned Up Philadelphia," *New Republic* No. 38, December 27, 1924; "Philadelphia's Amazing Defiance," *Colliers* No. 76, December 5, 1925. M. Jay Racusin and his King Canute simile are from the *New York Herald Tribune*, September 5, 1928. "Lawlessness was the price Philadelphia had to pay for what it wanted to drink," the *Colliers* article reckoned.

In addition to Lowell Thomas's *Old Gimlet Eye*, see Schmidt, Hans, *Maverick Marine: General Smedley D. Butler and the Contradictions of American Military History* (University Press of Kentucky, 1987). "Butler," wrote Schmidt, "came and went as a knight-errant whom everyone wished to use for disparate ends but no one wished to allow an enduring influence," page 159. For Butler's disputes with Carney and the origins of the Ritz-Carlton raid, see pages 155-157.

In one typical episode, Carney demanded publicly that Butler announce publicly that he (Butler) never actually heard him (Carney) allege publicly that the disgustingly sober Butler had attended "the 'drunkenest' party he (Carney) ever saw" on the night of Mayor Kendrick's election back in 1923. The "drunkenest party" allegation, as well as details of Old Gimlet Eye's departure, are from "Butler Is Packing Household Goods," *Philadelphia Inquirer*, December 12, 1925.

For the Venice Café ("Sure, we got beer"), see Arthur P. Dudden, *The City Embraces 'Normalcy' 1919-1929* in *Philadelphia – A 300-Year History.* See also Okrent, pp. 202-204 and 253; and Fred D. Baldwin, *Smedley D. Butler and Prohibition Enforcement in Philadelphia, 1924-1925,* in *Pennsylvania Magazine of History and Biography,* June 30, 1960. Baldwin sources the "100 per cent honest" quote to the *Evening Public Ledger,* December 23, 1925.

For the wine-drenched Piccadilly affair, see "Golder is Named as Participant in Piccadilly Orgy," *Philadelphia Inquirer,* November 16, 1928, page 1. For Butler's disdain for "jazzing up" young girls, see *Maverick Marine,* page 156. For Connie Mack's disavowal of Hughie as Smedley Butler's "smeller," see James Isaminger's "Hit and Run" column in the *Inquirer* of December 5, 1925, page 18.

The breathless report of Carney's inquiry into the Ritz-Carlton takedown appeared on the front page of the *Inquirer* on December 9, 1925: "Carney Enacts 'Poobah' Role in Ritz Hearing; Magistrate Sits as Judge, Prosecutor, and Witness in His Own 'Raid.'" The day's testimony, the paper said, was "replete with farcical scenes and burlesque wordy battles."

"A full quart of Scotch disappeared that night, with the cops," Carney alleged at one point.

"'Maybe the cops needed a little White Horse for their wagon,' Hughie McLoon interrupted from his place in the crowd, and the spectators again gave free vent to their mirth."

Chapter Thirteen

Officer Dean's actual assailant that night on Broad Street may have been a career criminal named Petey Ford, a.k.a. Forbes, a.k.a.

Grimmer, who had been acquitted of a murder charge in 1925 after serving time for highway robbery and other offenses. Ford, if that was his real name, was said to be a "distant relative" of Danny O'Leary. See *Philadelphia Inquirer,* September 5, 1926, page 2 and *Camden Courier,* August 18, 1926, "Former Mascot of A's Taken for Beating Cop."

Like the three titanic ring encounters of Muhammad Ali and Philadelphia's Joe Frazier a half-century later, the two Dempsey-Tunney fights were garbed in robes of brutality and skillfulness, patriotism and sedition, sophistication and social class. Writes Evensen: "Much seemed implied in the result." A single headline from the *Inquirer* encapsulated the tone: "Tunney's Clean-Cut Boxing Earns Him Coveted Heavyweight Title; Jack Wilts Under Fierce Attack of Fighting Marine."

See also, from the same edition of the same newspaper, September 24, 1926: "Big Throng Orderly in Rush on Stadium;" "New Fistic King is High in Praise of Fallen Heavy Champ;" Isaminger's "Fistic Pick-Ups Caught as Great Championship Battle Raged;" "Acre of Notables in Ringside Seats;" "Epidemic of Fights Precede Main Bout;" "Throngs Gay, Move Calmly, Despite Rain;" "Police Worn Out by Duties at Fight;" and "Women at Battle Most Ardent Fans." *The New York Times* devoted at least fifteen full pages to the fight.

Champion Tunney's engagement to Miss Mary "Polly" Lauder was made public on the same day that Hughie McLoon was killed. The two events monopolized the city's front pages: betrothal and betrayal.

For Odets, Kid Wagner, and the Automat, see Brenman-Gibson, Margaret, *Clifford Odets: American Playwright,* (Atheneum, 1981), p. 105.

For Hughie's activities in California, see *Los Angeles Times,* December 17, 1926 ("Wagner was forced to cancel several bouts that his manager, Hughie McLoon, had arranged here at local clubs"); "The Sock Basket," *San Francisco Examiner*, February 17 and 20, 1927; "Hughie McLoon said Brown was stale from too much boxing," March 6; "Cello Favorite in Bout with 'Kid' Wagner," March 29. Wagner fought 877 rounds as a professional, a life-sapping toll for a heavyweight. By comparison, Dempsey fought 284 rounds, Tunney 426, and Ali 548.

For Hoff's tinfoil artillery and more, see Desmond's 2003 monograph, "Remembering 'Boo Boo' Hoff" on The American Mafia web site: http://mafiahistory.us/a007/f_maxhoff.html

"'Scarface' Al Capone 'took it on the chin,'" reported the *Inquirer* on its front page of June 30, 1929, detailing Capone's arrest and Magistrate Carney's defiance. For more on Capone's confinement in the Greene Country Towne, see https://www.themarshallproject. org/2018/05/28/defending-al-capone

After McLoon's killing, Carney received a letter warning him "Your Next You Talk To Much," that was signed "Young Machine-Gun Men," *Philadelphia Inquirer*, August 18, 1928. For Capone's tenancy at Eastern State Penitentiary and more on Boo Boo Hoff, see Anderson, Anne Margaret and Binder, John J., *Philadelphia Organized Crime in the 1920s and 1930s* (Charleston, S. C., Arcadia Publishing, 2014.) "Philadelphia's corrupt culture–in which politicians and police could be bought and sold to protect common crooks and criminal dynasties–shaded how its citizens viewed lawbreakers," Anderson and Binder note, page 7.

As a young but already skyscraping pugilist, Ralph Smith sparred with Dempsey in Los Angeles. See Port Jervis (N.Y.) *Gazette,* March 25, 1922. For the McLoon-Ralph Smith partnership, see W. Rollo Wilson, "Eastern Snapshots," *Pittsburgh Courier*, May 16, 1925 and February 4, 1928 ("he sure can smear the rest of these bums");

Camden Evening Courier, September 27, 1927; *Philadelphia Inquirer,* October 19, 1927; *New York Evening Post,* November 9, 1927; *Inquirer* April 28, 1928.

"Boy wanted. Inquire at 927 Cuthbert St., today," read an ad in the *Inquirer* in 1909.

For the police raids on Ralph & Hughey's, see "Dry Raiders Find Swimming Pool Patrons All Wet," *Philadelphia Inquirer,* July 15, 1928, page 4; July 22, 1928, page 3. "No particular area was singled out by the squad," the newspaper asserted.

Chapter Fourteen

For the Rancocas hideaway, see "Gangsters' Lair in N. J. Woods Revealed By Girl," *Philadelphia Record,* August 29, 1928, Page 1. What appeared to be the same steep-roofed, two-story bunkhouse, now used as a stable, still stood under a large oak tree on the riverine site in December, 2019, just down an unpaved road from a community baseball diamond called "Field of Dreams."

For McLoon's alleged physical altercation with Doris Kearns, Ms. Kearns's putative employment at Rose Hicks's house of pleasure, the testimony of Magistrate Carney and Captain of Detectives Beckman, the gunmen's trip to New Jersey "for corn," and the other events that culminated in the fusillade on Cuthbert Street, there are innumerable and often wildly conflicting sources in addition to those cited above for Chapter One. See, for example, "Garage Man Held in McLoon Killing," *Evening Public Ledger,* August 17, 1928, page 1; "Hint Grossman Sought Revenge," *Evening Public Ledger,* October 1, 1928, page 6; "Death Car Driver Named By Beauty," *Evening Bulletin,* August 18, 1928.

For Dan O'Leary's previous arrests, see "Ward Shooting Suspect Is Freed," *Camden Courier*, June 22, 1925 and "Man is Wounded at Gunman's Home," *Philadelphia Inquirer*, June 4, 1927, page 3. For the "Bad Blood between O'Leary and McLoon Over a Girl," see *Camden Courier*, August 16, 1928, page 1.

For Virginia Fineman's role as "cloakroom girl," her malleable eyewitness account of the shootings, her confrontation with Elizabeth McLoon Geatens, and her "wild shrieks" at City Hall, see "Names Slain Gunman as McLoon Killer," *Philadelphia Record*, August 16, 1928, page 1; "'Cloak Room Girl' Lies, Says Carney," *Evening Bulletin,* September 3, 1928; "Cloakroom Girl Admits Naming O'Leary as Slayer," *Evening Bulletin*, September 4, 1928; "'Cloakroom Girl' Recants," *Evening Bulletin*, September 7, 1928.

For the vice raids of 1937, led by J. Edgar Hoover himself, that entangled the said Ms. Hicks and revivified the unsolved McLoon case, see "U. S. Vice Trials Open Here," *Camden Post*, November 16, 1937, page 1. ("McLoon is said to have manhandled Doris Kearns, now dead, at that time an inmate of the Hicks place.") Also see Gordon Mackay, "Is Zat So?" *Camden Evening Courier*, November 29, 1937 ("The white slave raids made last August by G-men under personal supervision of J. Edgar Hoover recalls the sensational killing of Hughie McLoon. . .") It was columnist Mackay who alleged that McLoon was "in his cups, often quarrelsome."

For the scene at the Jefferson Hospital and Judge Carney's statement that McLoon had come to him to announce that he was quitting the café, and the allegation that McLoon was to appear in court on August 10th in connection with the police raids on his saloon, see *Philadelphia Record*, August 10, 1928, page 5; "McLoon's Partner Named Murderers, Carney Declares," *Evening Bulletin*, August 31, 1928. For the mourners "in evening clothes" who "wept and swore," see *Chester Times*, August 9, 1928, page 1.

For a photo of the murder scene, see "Where Gangsters Killed One and Wounded Two," *Evening Bulletin*, August 9, 1928.

For the wounding, testimony, and recovery of Meister and Fries, see "Shot In McLoon Killing, Man Refuses to Talk," *Evening Public Ledger*, August 10, 1928; "Meister, Shot 13 Times, Grins at News of Arrests," *Evening Bulletin*, August 18, 1928; "Man Wounded by Slayers of M'Loon Held as Witness," *Evening Bulletin*, August 31, 1928.

In 1942, the self-same Meister was charged with receiving four fur coats stolen from a Walnut Street clothing store, "including a blood-stained Persian lamb wrapper." See "Blood Stains Mark Fur Seized in Home," *Philadelphia Inquirer*, October 6, 1942, page 23.

For Rabbi Cohen's impassioned sermon, see *The Jewish Exponent of Philadelphia*, Jewish Federation of Greater Philadelphia, September 21, 1928, page 16.

Chapter Fifteen

For the scene at 1508 Shunk Street and Mrs. Geatens's wailing at her first-born's graveside, see the notes to Chapter One and Fourteen, above, and "3,000 at McLoon Funeral," *The New York Times*, August 14, 1928, page 28.

For O'Leary's assassination, see "5 Gunmen Kill Man Sought in M'Loon Murder," *Evening Bulletin*, August 15, 1928; "Gangster Sought in Murder Slain," *The New York Times*, August 16, 1928, page 16; "New York 'Mob' is Blamed; 'Decoy Girl' Believed Here," *Evening Bulletin*, August 16, 1928; "Gunmen Have Murdered 25 Men Here in 3 Years," *Evening Bulletin*, August 16, 1928.

For Jennie Brooks's career as the alleged "decoy girl" in O'Leary's murder, see "Seek To Identify Girl as 'Decoy,'" *Evening Bulletin*, August 18, 1928; "Say Two Men Admit Aiding 'Decoy Girl' Rent Murder Room," *Evening Bulletin*, August 28, 1928; "Jennie Brooks Tells How Silent Guns Killed O'Leary," *Evening Bulletin*, August 31, 1928; "Jennie Describes Killing of O'Leary," *Evening Public Ledger*, August 31, 1928;

For O'Leary's farewell, see "10,000 View Body of Slain O'Leary," *Evening Bulletin*, August 20, 1928.

For Jennie Brooks's testimony and her exposure as Mrs. Anna Pechler Marcello, see "Jennie Brooks Faces Accusers," the *Evening Bulletin*, August 24, 1928; "Father Defends Jennie Brooks," Aug. 27; "Gang Had Glamour For Jennie Brooks," "'I'm Not Hard,' Wails Jennie Brooks, Held as 'Decoy' in O'Leary Killing," Aug. 28.

For the arrests of Grossman, Peterson, and Feldman and their courtroom *commedia*, see notes to Chapters One and Fifteen, above. See also "Peterson's Wife Pledges Loyalty" and "Girl Links Suspect With Gang Killings," both from *Philadelphia Evening Bulletin*, August 24, 1928, and "Girl Ties Peterson to O'Leary Murder as More Are Held," *Evening Public Ledger*, August 24, 1928. For Peterson's altercation with Detective Faries, see "Probers Think Arrests Will Clear Up Both Killings," *Evening Bulletin*, August 18, 1928.

For the shooting of Jim Daly, see "Boxer Shot Down . . . Defense of McLoon Believed Cause of Saloon Clash," *Philadelphia Inquirer*, August 19, 1928.

For the convening of the grand jury, see "Judge Directs Grand Jury Probe Gang Murders," *Philadelphia Evening Bulletin*, August 17, 1928. The lone woman on the panel, aptly enough, was named Sinn. See also "3 Held in Gang Deaths as Judge Orders Probe Into Organized Crime," *Philadelphia Inquirer*, August 18, 1928, page 1.

For the scene during the Grand Jury hearings, see "'Boo-Boo' Hoff Called In Probe of Gang Murders–Magistrate Carney Also Will Be Heard Today" and "Fight Manager Chief Witness of Day's Quiz," *Evening Bulletin,* August 21, 1928; "City Hall Agog Over Gang Probe–'Boo Boo' Mystery Man" and "Gunmen Convicts Confront 'Boo Boo' in Murder Probe," *Evening Bulletin,* August 22, 1928. For Petey Ford brought from Rockview Prison to face off with Boo Boo Hoff, see "Convicted Gunmen Confront Hoff in Grand Jury Room," *Philadelphia Inquirer,* August 23, 1928.

For the Grand Jury's findings, including excerpts from its report labeling Max Hoff as "boss bootlegger," see Haller, Mark H., "Philadelphia Bootlegging and the Report of the Special August Grand Jury," file:///C:/Users/Owner/Desktop/44049-Article%20Text-43888-1-10-20121205.pdf

For Mayor Mackey's dampened feelings, see *New York Herald Tribune,* September 5, 1928.

For Anna Marcello's liberation, see "Grants Freedom to Jennie Brooks–She Dances as She Leaves," *Evening Bulletin,* September 28, 1928. For her final appearance in the archives, see "Jennie Brooks Held on Visit to Husband," *Evening Bulletin,* May 12, 1934.

For Grossman's release, see "Automobile Top Man Discharged for Lack of Evidence in Hunchback's Slaying," *Evening Bulletin,* September 12, 1928. For the disposition of Peterson's case, see "Peterson Given Year Jail Term," *Evening Bulletin,* October 2, 1928

We last hear from Motor Top Man (and jealous lover of Doris Kearns?) Grossman in "Says 'Cards' Were Cheese Dumplings," *Evening Bulletin,* September 6, 1932. For the closing of the O'Leary murder case, see "Unable to Solve O'Leary Slaying," *Evening Bulletin,* December 20, 1928.

For the tragic ending to the life of the Dancing Judge, see "Ex-Magistrate Carney Killed in Auto Crash," *Philadelphia Inquirer,* February 2, 1941. For Connie Mack's final days and Red Smith's tribute, see Macht, Norman L., *The Grand Old Man of Baseball: Connie Mack in his Final Years, 1932-1956* (Lincoln, University of Nebraska Press, 2015).

For Shorty Feldman's long criminal career and his fortified death, see "'Shorty' Feldman, Suspect in Gang Killings, Freed," *Evening Bulletin,* October 11, 1928; "'Barbary Coast' Loses Liquor Permit," *Philadelphia Inquirer,* May 18, 1943; "Shorty Feldman Given 2 Years in Sale of Bonds," *Inquirer,* November 5, 1959; "Feldman Given 15-Mo. Term on Drug Charges," *Inquirer,* February 4, 1960; "Feldman's Body Released to Kin," *Inquirer,* September 12, 1960.

Epilogue

For the long mascotting career and melancholy demise of Eddie Bennett, see Leo Trachtenberg, "Eddie Bennett: Lucky Charm," *Yankees,* June 23, 1988; George Robinson and Margalit Fox, "Bat Boys," *The National Pastime: A Review of Baseball History,* Volume 10, Society for American Baseball Research, 1990; Smelser, Marshall, *The Life That Ruth Built* (New York, Quadrangle/New York Times Book Co., 1975); "Yankees Mascot Dies Amid Tokens," *The New York Times,* January 17, 1935; Yankees to Bury Mascot," *The New York Times,* January 18, 1935. Not a single Yankees player attended Bennett's mid-winter funeral.

For an account of the training accident that took Garth Garreau's life, see https://www.islandpacket.com/living/liv-columns-blogs/article33562062.html

For the rumored role of blackmail in Hughie's killing, see "$10,000 Extortion Hinted as Cause of M'Loon Murder," *Evening Bulletin*, December 6, 1928. For Gordon Mackay, see note to Chapter Fourteen, above. For George Dixon's report on Duffy's lavish contribution to Hughie's wake, see "Well, That's Washington," *Albany Times-Union*, April 27, 1947.

"The past alone is truly real," Russell wrote in *On History*. "The present is but a painful, struggling birth into the immutable being of what is no longer. Only the dead exist fully. The lives of the living are fragmentary, doubtful, and subject to change; but the lives of the dead are complete, free from the sway of Time, the all-but omnipotent lord of the world."